W9-AAX-435

Women in the Arts

Sarah Bernhardt

Coco Chanel

Agnes de Mille

Dorothea Lange

Nina Simone

Virginia Woolf

Coco Chanel

He who neglects the arts when he is young
has lost the past and is dead to the future.

—Sophocles, *Fragments*

WOMEN in the ARTS

Coco Chanel

Ann Gaines

Introduction by
Congresswoman Betty McCollum
Minnesota, Fourth District
Member, National Council on the Arts

CHELSEA HOUSE
PUBLISHERS
A Haights Cross Communications Company
Philadelphia

CHELSEA HOUSE PUBLISHERS

VP, NEW PRODUCT DEVELOPMENT Sally Cheney
DIRECTOR OF PRODUCTION Kim Shinners
CREATIVE MANAGER Takeshi Takahashi
MANUFACTURING MANAGER Diann Grasse

Staff for COCO CHANEL

EDITOR Patrick M. N. Stone
PRODUCTION ASSISTANT Megan Emery
ASSISTANT PHOTO EDITOR Noelle Nardone
SERIES & COVER DESIGNER Terry Mallon
LAYOUT 21st Century Publishing and Communications, Inc.

©2004 by Chelsea House Publishers,
a subsidiary of Haights Cross Communications.
All rights reserved. Printed and bound in the United States of America.

A Haights Cross Communications ✦ Company

www.chelseahouse.com

First Printing

1 3 5 7 9 8 6 4 2

Library of Congress Cataloging-in-Publication Data

Gaines, Ann.
    Coco Chanel/by Ann Gaines.
        p. cm.—(Women in the arts)
Includes index.
Summary: A biography of the innovative twentieth-century designer
of clothing and perfume.
    ISBN 0-7910-7455-2 (Hardcover)   0-7910-7950-3 (PB)
    1. Chanel, Coco, 1883-1971—Juvenile literature. 2. Women fashion
designers—France—Biography—Juvenile literature. 3. Costume
design—France—History—20th century—Juvenile literature.
[1. Chanel, Coco, 1883-1971. 2. Fashion designers. 3. Women—
Biography.] I. Title. II. Series: Women in the arts (Philadelphia, Pa.)
TT505.C45G356 2003
746.9'2'092—dc21
                                                         2003009482

Table of Contents

Introduction

Congresswoman Betty McCollum
Minnesota, Fourth District
Member, National Council on the Arts

I am honored to introduce WOMEN IN THE ARTS, a continuing series of books about courageous, talented women whose work has changed the way we think about art and society. The women highlighted in this series were persistent, successful, and at times controversial. They were unafraid to ask questions or challenge social norms while pursuing their work. They overcame barriers that included discrimination, prejudice, and poverty. The energy, creativity, and perseverance of these strong women changed our world forever.

Art plays a critical role in all our lives, in every culture, and especially in the education of young people. Art can be serious, beautiful, functional, provocative, spiritual, informative, and illuminating. For all of the women in this series, their respective forms of artistic expression were a creative exploration and their professional calling. Their lives and their work transformed the world's perception of a woman's role in society.

In reading this series, I was struck by common themes evident in these women's lives that can provide valuable lessons for today's young women.

One volume tells the story of Coco Chanel, the first fashion designer to create clothing for women that was both attractive and utile. Chanel was one of the first women to run a large, successful business in the fashion industry. Today, it is hard to imagine the controversy Chanel stirred up simply by making women's clothing beautiful, comfortable, and practical. Chanel understood that women wanted a sense of style and professionalism in their fashion, as men had in theirs.

Chanel's extraordinary success demonstrates that we should not be afraid to be controversial. Even today, women of all ages worry far too much about stepping on toes or questioning authority. To make change, in our own lives or in our community, we need to stand up and speak out for our beliefs. The women of this series often defied convention and ruffled some feathers, but they never stopped. Nina Simone sang beautifully, but she also spoke out against the injustice of racism, regardless of how it affected her career.

It is equally important for us women to ask ourselves, "What do I want from my life?" We all struggle to answer this deceptively simple question. It takes courage to answer it honestly, but it takes far more courage to answer the question and then *act* on that answer. For example, Agnes de Mille realized she had "nothing to lose by being direct." She stuck to her vision for *Rodeo,* insisted on the set and composer she envisioned, and eventually produced her ballet—the way she wanted to. She believed in her vision, and the result was a great success. Dorothea Lange, having decided she wanted to become a photographer, asked for photography jobs, even though she had no experience and it was a profession that few women pursued.

In our society, we expect that all people should be treated with respect and dignity, but this has not always been true. Nina Simone faced discrimination and overcame social norms that promoted racial injustice. She confronted prejudice and disrespect directly, sometimes refusing to perform when an audience was unruly or rude. One evening, when she was only eleven years old, she even delayed her performance until her own parents were allowed to sit in the front row—seats that they had been asked to vacate for white people. Her demand for respect took courage.

Women's equality not only benefits women, but also brings a unique perspective to the world. For example, the brilliance of Dorothea Lange's photography was in large part due to her empathy for her subjects. She knew that to tell their story, she needed to earn their trust and to truly understand their lives.

Each of these women used her art to promote social justice. Coco Chanel used her designs to make women's lives easier and more comfortable, while Nina Simone was as committed to civil rights as she was to her music. Dorothea Lange's photographs convinced Washington of the need to establish sanitary camps for migrant families, and Virginia Woolf's writing pushed the question of equal rights for women.

Because the women in these books, and so many others like them, took risks and challenged society, women today have more opportunity than ever before. We have access to equal education, and we are making great strides in the workplace and in government.

As only the second woman from Minnesota ever elected to serve in Congress, I know how important it is to have strong female role models. My grandmothers were born in a time when women did not have the right to vote, but their granddaughter is now a Member of Congress. Their strength, wisdom, and courage inspire me. Other great women, such as Congresswoman Barbara Jordan and Congresswoman Shirley Chisholm, also inspired me with their leadership and determination to overcome gender and racial discrimination to serve in Congress with distinction.

Dorothea Lange once said, "I have learned from everything, and I'm constantly learning." I know that I too am constantly learning. I hope the women in this series will inspire you to learn and to lead with courage and determination. Art, as a profession or a hobby, can be either an expression or an agent of change. We need to continue to encourage women to add their voices to our society through art.

The women profiled in this series broke barriers, followed their hearts, refused to be intimidated, and changed our world. Their lives and successes should be a lesson to women everywhere. In addition, and importantly, they created lasting and meaningful art. I hope that you will enjoy this series as much as I have.

1

Le Comeback

A style does not go out of style as long as it adapts itself to its period. When there is an incompatibility between the style and a certain state of mind, it is never the style that triumphs.

—Coco Chanel, quoted in Marcel Haedrich's
Coco Chanel: Her Life, Her Secrets

On February 5, 1954, Coco Chanel returned to the world of fashion after an exile of 15 years. She perched unseen on a stairway during the event, watching the audience in the mirrored showroom below from between the rails of a banister. Everyone who mattered in fashion had turned out, and socialites and editors from fashion magazines sat on the gilded chairs, watching Chanel's models parade down the runway. The first model wore a navy-blue suit that Chanel had kept extremely simple, refusing to add

Coco Chanel in 1954. She had revolutionized women's fashion for 30 years before disappearing from public life at the start of World War II. Now, 15 years later, she was back—and her new collections would reestablish her as the industry's leading designer.

even a collar to its jacket. Similar plain pieces followed.

Generally, attendees of a fashion show chatter among themselves and point out to one another the pieces they like best. Sometimes they rise and applaud. But this was not the case with Chanel's comeback show: According to observer Michael Deon, Chanel's audience remained still and silent throughout, and at the end a few people called the show a waste of their time.

The reviews that appeared in French newspapers the next day were derogatory. Chanel's foremost biographer, Edmonde Charles-Roux, wrote, "The French press was revoltingly vulgar, stupid, and nasty. There were gibes at her age." (365) Reviewers regarded Chanel, then 70 years old, as being as hopelessly outdated as her work. They predicted that none of her plain but expensive little suits would find buyers.

Chanel remained calm and collected in public, and on February 6, the day after the show, she went right back to work on a new collection. Pierre Wertheimer, her business associate, tried to talk her out of it—he wanted to spare himself the expense, and her the humiliation, of another failure—but she convinced him that the naysayers were wrong and that her clothing would indeed be a success. Department stores and salons, notified that she was back in business, had ordered stock from her months earlier. Despite the bad press she had received, they would display her new line. This, Chanel knew, was the true test. She would be proven right.

•   •   •   •

In 1953, Chanel had returned from exile in Switzerland to the fashionable Rue Cambon in Paris to re-open her *maison de couture*, her boutique that, for 15 years, had sold her signature perfume and accessories. It was one of the biggest risks of her life.

Born illegitimate and poor, she had her first chance at success in her mid-twenties, when a lover gave her the money to open a tiny millinery. Coming of age in an era when fashion compelled women to wear tight corsets and bustles under their clothing, she defied the dictates of her time and started to design simple and comfortable, yet beautiful, clothes that were extremely popular with women. For decades, fashion magazines featured her designs, and she was credited more than once with revolutionizing women's fashion. Through decades of hard work, Chanel built from that humble beginning a successful business that employed thousands of women. By the late 1930s, Coco Chanel had become one of the world's leading *couturières*.

She had also become extremely famous. Her name appeared frequently in gossip columns and reports on the modern art scene. Not only was she a friend of many of the world's greatest artists, but she had affairs with some of the world's most powerful men over the years, including the duke of Westminster, England's wealthiest aristocrat. By 1939, though, she left the limelight. When World War II began and the Germans were expected to invade France, Chanel decided to stop designing clothes and dismissed her staff. Detractors accused her of having wanted to do so for several years, ever since her seamstresses had offended her by striking for better wages and working conditions. She claimed that she was closing her business only to prevent its being seized by the Germans and used for their benefit.

For years afterward, she led a very quiet life, continuing to live at the first-class Hôtel Ritz in German-occupied Paris, as she had before the war. In the mid-1940s she fled the city; this may well have been because of rumors that were circulating at the time that she was a Nazi sympathizer—for she had had a love affair during the war with a rich German businessman who had turned out to be a high-ranking intelligence officer. She moved from Paris to Switzerland, where she lived in the obscurity of a self-imposed exile.

Her life of seclusion began to bore her, though, and she dreamed of working again, trusting that what had happened during the war would no longer interest people. She despised the current fashions. Christian Dior, the reigning designer of the day, used yards upon yards of sumptuous fabric to create elaborate dresses featuring wide skirts and tiny waists that he achieved through tight bodices and constrictive boning. Chanel hated Dior's ostentation. She wanted to pick up her favorite tool, her scissors, and snip away at soft fabric, to once again create clothing in which a woman could move freely while looking good. Yet again, she had in mind a whole new look.

CHANEL, DIOR, AND THE NEW LOOK

Chanel biographers have suggested several reasons for her return to fashion after 15 years of seclusion. One possibility is that she objected to the designs that were popular at the time—that she felt that women needed to be liberated once again. If this is true, then she may have been particularly opposed to the designs of rival designer Christian Dior.

In 1947, Dior had proposed what the magazine *Harper's Bazaar* had dubbed the "New Look." These designs included a full, pleated calf-length skirt and a fitted jacket, which was belted tightly to form a tiny waist; they seemed to be resurrecting the ideas of femininity that were current before World War I and before Chanel. The New Look emphasized the waist and upper body while totally obscuring the hips, and it was often complemented by gloves and brimmed hats. It was a celebration of the end of wartime rationing; Dior's outfits used far more fabric than had been called for in any of Chanel's designs. "My dream," said Dior of female beauty in 1955, "is to save [women] from nature." Chanel's vision of femininity had always been very different—stronger, sleeker, more active and energetic, more natural. The New Look was immensely popular at the time and came to typify the female figure of the 1950s and early 1960s. It now seems dated, though, whereas Chanel's classic lines have never lost their appeal.

Staunchly determined to ignore any negative comments, she returned to Paris and reopened her *maison de couture*. She hired 300 employees, all of whom worked feverishly for six months in her workrooms, following her orders, to prepare her new collection. This is the collection that was so coldly received in 1954.

But Chanel had faith in her work, even after the harsh reviews, and she believed that its popularity would grow. She was right; slowly in Europe, but much more quickly in the United States, women began to pay high prices for the clothing that Chanel had designed, and soon they were demanding more of the same. New orders poured in.

Her second comeback collection was received much more favorably than the first. In early 1955, *Life* magazine put Chanel on its cover, reporting that she had started a revolution in women's fashion by creating clothing that the successful woman of the day could actually wear. As Karl Lagerfeld, the heir to the Chanel label, put it, "By the '50s, she had the benefit of distance, and so could truly distill the Chanel look. Time and culture had caught up with her." (Sischy, 3)

From that point on, Chanel's sales grew. Women continued to love the once-disparaged suits, which she reworked hundreds of times. Soft and untailored, they always featured a boxy cardigan jacket without a collar and a straight, knee-length skirt with a slit in the back that allowed the wearer to stand up and sit down easily, to get in and out of cars gracefully, and to walk about naturally. Paying close attention to even the tiniest details, Chanel made sure that every suit had pockets and sleeves with buttons that were not just decorative but also functional.

To go along with her suits, she designed beautifully draped blouses, shoulder bags, and two-toned pumps. She also designed sportswear and evening outfits that were flattering and similarly luxurious in feel. The look that Chanel created remains popular among the most affluent and powerful women of today.

Chanel reviewing a dress from her new collection, 1957. By this time, Chanel had survived the cold reception of her first comeback collection and regained her prewar popularity. Younger designers were making their way in the fashion world, but Chanel was still the trend-setter, known both for the celebrities she dressed and for the many imitators of her work.

Her comeback, once the object of ridicule, is today considered to have been a complete success. For almost two decades more, until her death in 1971, Chanel remained the world's leading fashion designer. She was hailed as one of the most influential women of her time. The government of France considered her one of that nation's best emissaries. When she died, obituaries appeared in major newspapers all over the globe. Her estate was revealed to be worth hundreds of millions in American dollars.

Now, more than 30 years after her death, her business continues to grow. Her *maison de couture*, run by designer Karl Lagerfeld, remains a trendsetter and ranks among the most successful in the world. In 2001, *Time* magazine, having listed her among the 100 most influential people of the twentieth century, summed up the reason for her success: "The clothes she created changed the way women looked and how they looked at themselves." (Sischy, 1)

2

The Mystery of Chanel's Early Years

1883–1903

A child in revolt becomes a person with armor and strength. It's the kisses, caresses, teachers, and vitamins that kill children and turn them into unhappy or sickly adults. It's the mean and the nasty aunts who create whiners, and give them inferiority complexes, although in my case the result was a superiority complex. Under nastiness looms strength, under pride a taste for success and a passion for grandeur.

—Coco Chanel, quoted in Axel Madsen's
Chanel: A Woman of Her Own

By the time Coco Chanel died, in 1971, she was known the world over as an immensely wealthy fashion designer who had made a fortune from her signature perfume, *Chanel No. 5*, and the many styles she had introduced. For years she had moved with grace and ease in the world of the rich and the famous. She was accustomed to exchanging ideas with some of the most

The town of Saumur. Saumur has been home to France's national cavalry school since the eighteenth century; the school trains some of the world's most accomplished horses and riders and employs top veterinarians. It was in Saumur that Albert Chanel sold corsets, Jeanne Devolle struggled to make ends meet, and Gabrielle Chanel was born. The town also has a history of quartering the soldiers whose uniforms may have inspired Chanel's early designs.

creative minds of her time, including the composer Igor Stravinsky and the painter Pablo Picasso.

This was dramatically different from the life of her early years. When she had begun to rise, as an adult, in social circles, Chanel had created for herself a legend; little of what she said about her past to friends, staff, and reporters was the truth. In the words of journalist Ingrid Sischy, she frequently hid the harsh truth and resorted to "lies, inventions, cover-ups, and revisions." (Sischy, 1) In short, Chanel's tales of her own life were largely a work of art.

Even though she tried to obscure the facts about her early years, though, Chanel's biographers have discovered details about her immensely difficult childhood, along with information about her private life as an adult that she did not want known. She may have covered up some of this information from social pressures—like her affair with a Nazi officer during World War II—but she was equally secretive about her good deeds, such as her financial support of artists in financial trouble.

To this day, many sources, including the Chanel Company, present as fact what Coco Chanel wanted people to believe. This makes it difficult to determine with any certainty exactly what happened in her life, especially before the public began to keep track of her. Some facts can be verified, though, and sensible speculations can be made.

THE DISPUTED ORIGINS OF THE CHANEL FAMILY

Chanel cited different years for her birth, trying at times to present herself as younger than she was. Nevertheless, church records bear out that Gabrielle Chanel—who would later be nicknamed Coco—was born on August 19, 1883, in the town of Saumur, France, located southwest of Paris. As an adult, Chanel claimed that godparents had given her the middle name Bonheur, which translates as "happiness," but this name does not appear on her baptismal certificate. Her parents were Albert Chanel and Jeanne Devolle, an unmarried couple; Albert was the oldest son in a large and scattered family.

Over the years, Chanel told friends many different stories about her family's origin. In her old age, she claimed she was from a family of "good stock" (Baillèn, 169), by which she meant that her family was settled and well-to-do. She painted a rosy picture of a family with servants that lived in a large house in the country near Nîmes and vacationed in Vichy, a spa town in central France.

Biographer Edmonde Charles-Roux later refuted these claims. Doing research for the book entitled, in English, *Chanel: Her Life, Her World, and the Woman Behind the Legend She Herself Created*, Charles-Roux tracked down Chanel's surviving distant relations, who confirmed that she was in fact raised in poverty in what today would be described as a dysfunctional family. They told Charles-Roux their family came from the Cévennes, a rocky mountain range in southern France.

According to these relatives, Albert's grandfather had owned a tavern in the tiny farming village of Ponteils. Every year, the families of Ponteils went into the surrounding forests to gather chestnuts which, when roasted, are a very popular snack in France. When the chestnut trees of Ponteils became diseased and there was no crop to be gathered and sold, the townspeople could no longer afford to visit Albert's grandfather's tavern. Financially ruined, the Chanel family had to leave Ponteils.

At first the young Henri-Adrien, Albert's father, worked as a farmhand outside the town of Travers de Castillon. He did not hold this job long before he was fired for conceiving a child with the farmer's 16-year-old daughter, Angelina. To save face, they hastily married and then fled the town.

Henri-Adrien and Angelina became peddlers. France was then, as now, a predominantly Catholic country. The church calendar is crowded with saints' days. Henri-Adrien and Angelina walked from town to town, selling cheap goods, such as handkerchiefs, at the annual fairs held to celebrate the days dedicated to the local churches' patron saints.

When Angelina reached the end of her pregnancy, Henri-Adrien left her at a charity hospital in the city of Nîmes and went right back out on the road to earn some desperately needed money. Angelina gave birth to Albert. Illiterate, she could not fill out his birth record; a hospital official had to do this for her and in the process misspelled their surname as Charnet.

As soon as she was able to travel, Angelina reunited with Henri-Adrien. Albert and the younger brothers and sisters who would follow spent their childhood on the road with their parents, sometimes staying with other members of the Chanels' extended family. On one or two occasions, Albert and his closest sibling, his sister Louise, were able to go to school for a few months during the winter. As the family grew in size and there were more mouths to feed, schooling ceased and the older children had to work every day—either as day laborers, haying or picking grapes for farmers, or hawking wares in the streets.

When Albert was in his early teens, he struck out on his own. He enlisted in the army for one term, but he did not want a career in the military. After his enlistment ended, he bought a supply of wine and traveled throughout France to sell it. As the winter of 1881 began, he stopped for a time in the small town of Courpière and rented a room in the house of a young carpenter named Marin Devolle. Albert Chanel and Marin Devolle became friends.

In the months that followed, Albert began a romance with Devolle's 19-year-old sister, Jeanne, who lived in the same town with an uncle. Their relationship became intimate, and Jeanne hoped that Albert would propose, but he refused to marry her. When Albert left, soon after New Year's, Jeanne was pregnant. The uncle with whom she was living, a businessman, learned of her pregnancy and was scandalized enough to throw her out of his house. Jeanne took refuge with Marin, who enlisted the help of town officials to find Albert.

The authorities did eventually locate Albert's parents. They told his mother that Albert risked being arrested and sentenced to hard labor in a work camp if he did not take responsibility for the child, and she revealed his where-abouts. It was not the police but Jeanne who sought and found the reluctant Albert in the village of Aubenas. He still refused to marry her, but he did agree to recognize the child as his own and to let Jeanne share his room at the inn in which he was living.

On September 11, 1882, Jeanne gave birth to a girl named Julia—Gabrielle's older sister. Chanel would later claim that they were six years apart in age; in reality, only one year separated them.

THE INSTABILITY OF CHANEL'S CHILDHOOD

Following Julia's birth, Albert left Jeanne once more. The tenacious Jeanne followed and caught up to him in the Loire River Valley, in the town of Saumur, where many units of the French cavalry were headquartered. Riding their fine horses through the streets, wearing uniforms trimmed in braid and decorated with gilt buttons, the soldiers made Saumur an exciting place to live. There were many restaurants, cafes, and taverns to serve the soldiers, and the shops that normally closed at dusk in other small French towns stayed open late into the night in Saumur.

Life in Saumur was hardly glamorous or exciting for Jeanne. Living with Albert in a bare, cold garret in a dilapidated house in a poor part of town, she became pregnant again. Sometimes Albert set up a booth in Saumur's open-air market and sold corsets and other types of ladies' undergarments, but he often went on the road, leaving Jeanne behind. She did her part to support the family, although what sort of work she did can only be guessed. She probably found work as a cleaning woman or laundress. She stopped working only when she went into labor, giving birth to a second girl on August 19, 1883. Albert was away at the time, but Jeanne made sure his name appeared as father on the birth record of the daughter. She named the child Gabrielle—the future Coco Chanel.

Ladies' undergarments in the nineteenth century. Gabrielle Chanel's father, Albert, sold items like these—corsets, bustles, petticoats—in the open-air markets of Saumur and elsewhere, and the elaborate style of dress at the time made the corset trade very lucrative. Albert made a precarious living from these garments, but his daughter's designs would eliminate them forever.

Little is known of Gabrielle's early years. Biographer Charles-Roux believes Jeanne and the girls lived for a full year in Saumur and states that this would be the longest they would remain in one place. Albert continued to rove, earning his living as an itinerant salesman. When both girls were old enough to travel, they and Jeanne sometimes went with him. Other times she stayed behind in a town where she could work for a time as a seamstress or maid.

In the winter of 1884, the family spent some time in Jeanne's hometown of Courpière, where Albert and Jeanne finally were married on November 17, 1884. A formal commitment to Jeanne did not make Albert spend more time with his family, though. He continued to travel, often without them. In 1885, Jeanne gave birth to their first son. This did not change Albert's ways, either. The couple would have one more daughter and two more sons, the last of whom died as a baby.

The situation remained the same for several years. Then, in 1893, Albert wrote to Jeanne from Brive-la-Gaillarde. He had stopped peddling, at least for a time, to take a job in an inn where his brother worked, as a waiter. By this time, Gabrielle was ten years old. She and Julia must already have become accustomed to working, either helping Albert to sell goods in a market or helping Jeanne scrub laundry or clean the homes of the wealthy. With their parents always struggling to make money, the children often must have been cold and hungry. Rarely, if ever, would they have lived in a clean, dry, warm house. They probably never had a chance to go to school—certainly not consistently.

By this time, Jeanne had become very ill. Coco Chanel's friend Claude Baillèn, who wrote a biography of Chanel after her death, writes that Chanel told him her mother had died of tuberculosis (Baillèn, 167); but Chanel may have told him this merely because it was a romantic story. Jeanne did have asthma, according to Charles-Roux, but the cause of her death was probably simply exhaustion and overwork. Jeanne died on February 16, 1895, at the age of 33.

THE ORPHANAGE AT AUBAZINE

Albert was traveling when Jeanne died. His brother Hippolyte made arrangements to have her buried and he looked after the children until Albert returned. When Albert finally did come back, he quickly decided he would no longer consider himself responsible for the children.

Chanel later told Claude Baillèn that Albert took Julia to a convent but left *her*, his favorite child, with some aged aunts in Auvergne while he went to the United States to make his fortune. According to Charles-Roux, the truth is different: Albert took Gabrielle and her sisters Julia and Antoinette to an orphanage run by nuns in Aubazine and sent their brothers to work for farmers. Charles-Roux writes that Albert himself then returned to his life as a peddler and never again made an effort to see his children.

In some ways, life at the orphanage in Aubazine must have been easier than the life to which Gabrielle had been accustomed. After all, the nuns saw that their charges were always fed and clothed and had warm, dry beds. They also provided education, teaching their students to read, write, and perform simple calculations, instructing them in skills such as sewing, and providing them with religious training. Some nuns may have been kind, but the majority were probably severe. They would have supervised the girls closely, making sure the girls had little time to themselves. It was probably only rarely that Gabrielle had an opportunity simply to play.

Unless they had decided to take vows and become nuns themselves, girls at the convent remained at Aubazine only until they approached the age of 18; so, when Gabrielle was 17, the nuns sent her and Julia to a school in Moulins, a lively city in the center of France. Antoinette would later follow.

The town hall of Moulins. Like Saumur, Moulins ("Windmills") has a history of quartering soldiers and it is by singing poorly to these enthusiasts that Chanel acquired the nickname "Coco." Chanel also began her close relationship with her aunt Adrienne while the two were at school together in Moulins, and while working as a seamstress with Adrienne she began to do her own alterations. This photograph was taken around 1900.

Charles-Roux thinks their father's sister may have requested that they be sent there, since she lived just 12 miles outside of Moulins, in the village of Varennes. (Charles-Roux, 47)

In Moulins, Gabrielle continued her strictly controlled education, but one thing there brought her great joy. By happenstance, Gabrielle's aunt Adrienne Chanel was attending the same school. She and Gabrielle were the same age. Adrienne was a lively girl. She and Gabrielle became close friends and would remain so for many years. Many even thought they were sisters.

While in Moulins, the Chanel girls also came to know other members of their extended family. Their father's sister, their aunt Julia, did in fact invite the girls to come and stay with her family in Varennes from time to time. She had elevated her station in life from lower- to middle-class by marrying a railroad man, and with her husband she led a much more stable life than that of Albert and Jeanne.

Gabrielle never formed a particularly close relationship with Julia, but she may have learned an important skill from her: millinery. In that age, most Americans and Europeans wore hats whenever they left the house, and huge hats decorated with feathers, flowers, and elaborate trims were in vogue for French women. Julia is believed to have made a special annual trip to a large city to buy her hats, which she would then trim herself. According to one version of Chanel's introduction to millinery, Julia taught her nieces to trim hats, as well.

CHANEL AND THE SOLDIERS

When they turned 19, Gabrielle and Adrienne left school. (Julia had already left and was working for an uncle.) The nuns helped them to find lodging and employment sewing in a tailor's shop in Moulins. Although Gabrielle, who sewed well, eventually began doing alterations on her own, she had higher ambitions and did not plan to spend the rest of her life as a seamstress. She had always enjoyed singing in the church choir, and her voice, though thin, had been praised; she dreamed of a career on the stage, as a singer, but she had not yet actively pursued this dream.

In the late nineteenth century, many cavalry and infantry regiments of the French army were stationed in the large and bustling city of Moulins. Many officers in both branches of the military were dandies, the sons of aristocrats or merchants, and had money to spend. One day, a group of cavalrymen came into the shop in which Gabrielle and Adrienne worked as seamstresses. As the officers were leaving their uniforms for mending, they glimpsed the girls behind the counter; they lingered outside until the Chanel girls finished work and then approached them. In the months that followed, both girls spent much of their free time with these soldiers and others. Gabrielle developed a romance with an infantry officer named Étienne Balsan.

The soldiers often invited the girls to go with them to cafés and cabarets, or nightclubs. These places advertised well-known performers, but they also allowed *poseuses* to take the stage from time to time. These always young, always pretty women sat onstage and took turns singing whenever the headliner needed a break. The custom was for the cabaret owner to pay the girls nothing but to permit them to pass a hat after their song to collect tips from the audience.

Gabrielle became a *poseuse* at an establishment called La Rotonde. In truth, despite her fantasies of becoming a singer, she did not have much of a voice. Nevertheless, her male friends came especially to see her and they spent money on drinks and cigarettes, and so the owner of La Rotonde liked her well enough. She also lacked a repertoire, knowing only the two popular songs "Ko Ko Ri Ko" and "Qui A Vu Coco dans le Trocadéro?" When she finished one of her two songs, her fans roared in delight and urged her to repeat the performance by shouting "Coco! Coco!"—and soon enough, according to one of the several versions, Coco became her nickname. From about the age of 20 onward, she referred to herself as Coco Chanel and stopped using her given name, Gabrielle.

Coco continued to sew during the day and sing at night, with her usual success, and eventually she began to think of trying her luck farther afield. She decided to try to earn a living as a singer in Vichy, a wealthy spa town located about 30 miles away. There, the upper classes visited the hot springs to "take the water," meaning they took mud baths and drank the spring water in the hope of improving their health. Adrienne agreed to go along. Her soldier paramour Étienne Balsan gave Coco money for clothes and a railway ticket. He also visited her in Vichy.

Coco auditioned at a nightclub in Vichy but was not

THE CABARET

C oco Chanel grew up during the period in European history that francophones call the Belle Epoque (the Beautiful Era) and anglophones the Gilded Age (ca. 1875–1915). Certainly, neither of these names applied for poor families like hers, who struggled to earn enough for basic necessities, such as food and clothing. French society included not just a large number of working-class people, but a large group of rich and privileged people as well.

During the Belle Epoque, a favorite pursuit for wealthy men was visiting a cabaret at night, where they drank and flirted with women. The cabaret in Moulins in which Chanel sang—one of two in the town—was probably very typical of those in towns and smaller cities: A number of scantily clad women sat on a stage and struck suggestive poses as one of their number came forward to sing either a love song or a more risqué piece rich in double entendres. Chanel got her start as a *poseuse*, as these women were called, but she was eventually given the chance to sing, too.

In Paris there were much bigger cabarets, like the Folies Bergères, that put on lavish floor shows similar to those depicted in the Baz Luhrmann film *Moulin Rouge!* (2001), which is set around the time of Chanel's childhood. The scandalous Moulin Rouge is still in operation. The Bob Fosse film *Cabaret* (1972) explores a similar theme but is set in Germany during the rise of the Nazi regime.

offered a job. Following a professional's advice, she took singing lessons, rented a costume, and continued to look for work. But it was all to no avail; she was never offered a contract to sing, and after a season she returned to Moulins. She'd been there for only a short time before Balsan offered her a new life. His stint in the army was about to end and he was leaving Moulins to live on an estate he had just purchased in Compiègne, just north of Paris. He invited her to live with him as his mistress. This meant she would no longer have to support herself, and she accepted his offer.

3

Chanel Goes into Business

1904–1914

The hat is not for the street: it will never be democratized. But there are certain houses that one cannot enter without a hat. And one must always wear a hat when lunching with people whom one does not know well. One appears to one's best advantage.

—Coco Chanel, quoted in Marcel Haedrich's
Coco Chanel: Her Life, Her Secrets

Elegance is not the prerogative of those who have just escaped from adolescence, but of those who have already taken possession of their future.

—Coco Chanel, quoted in *McCall's*, November 1965

Balsan could be described as a *bon vivant*, a liver of the good life, a person whose own amusement often takes priority over all other concerns. Raised in an upper-middle-class family, he inherited enough money when his parents died to buy

34

Chanel in 1910. Chanel developed a romance with an infantry officer, Étienne Balsan, and was eventually invited to live with him as his mistress at Royallieu, which she did for several years. This photograph shows Chanel as she was stepping out of life at Royallieu, ready to pursue more fulfilling and meaningful projects.

himself the country estate in Compiègne, named Royallieu, in December of 1904. This was a large piece of property, which included an expansive château, stables, and other farm buildings surrounded by fields and woods.

Balsan moved to Royallieu when his enlistment period ended and he left the army. He set to work to establish a stud farm, buying stallions with good bloodlines that he would mate with mares in return for a fee paid by the mares' wealthy owners. He also planned to ride horses in steeplechase races across open countryside or over obstacle courses. He loved this sport mostly for the thrill it gave him. Money was not a grave concern to him, so he pursued his career as a horseman more out of personal interest than financial necessity.

When Balsan invited Chanel to leave Moulins and live with him at Royallieu as his mistress, neither of them seem to have expected a permanent relationship. Balsan had no intention of making Chanel mistress of the château; it was always clearly *his* house, not theirs. To keep an *irregulière*, a mistress, was common practice among rich Frenchmen. Courtesans, or women kept by very wealthy men, had been part of the life of the privileged minority for centuries. Many men, like Balsan, supported their mistresses, paying all their bills. Some were wealthy enough to have more than one mistress, and it was said that Coco Chanel was not even Balsan's *primary* mistress, but a backup among others. He is believed to have kept another woman in Paris, presumably in a grander style.

Balsan and Chanel were never alone in the house. He had a staff of several servants, including a cook, a valet, and a maid, who saw to the needs of a steady stream of houseguests who stayed for days, even weeks, at a time. Many guests brought their own mistresses along. All of Balsan's friends had one interest in common—they loved to ride horses. A "merry band of mates," they lived a life without care. In the worlds of Charles-Roux, aside from "horses, laughter, and pleasure," they cared for nothing. (Charles-Roux, 87)

AN EARLY INNOVATION: THE RIDING HABIT

When she first arrived, Chanel did not share Balsan's enjoyment of horses. After all, she'd had no opportunity to be around horses when she was a child. But Balsan soon taught her to ride horseback and ignited in her a passion like his. Chanel not only greatly enjoyed riding, but excelled at it. From that point on, she rode both alone and with Balsan and his friends. They spent many weekends hunting on horseback.

In the neighborhood of Royallieu, there lived many wealthy women who rode horses for sport, and most of the female guests at Royallieu rode, too. Chanel stood out among them, thanks in large part to her riding outfit. Although Balsan supported her, giving her lodging and food, he apparently did not offer her much pocket money or buy her many expensive presents, and she had to buy her own riding clothes. In that era, French women typically rode sidesaddle, wearing long, heavy skirts and small, tight jackets. Chanel disliked such riding habits because they were very expensive and the skirts prevented her from riding astride. For her own riding habits, then, she went not to the local dressmaker but to a tailor who made men's clothes. He made for her a pair of jodhpurs, leather pants that ended just below the knee. She wore these with a loose shirt, which she left open at the collar, and a scarf. She did this out of personal style, but Balsan loved the effect, and he showed her off to his friends more and more frequently.

Balsan and Chanel spent most of their days at Royallieu, riding and entertaining friends, but they occasionally made quick visits to Paris. They spent a little time shopping there, but they went to Paris primarily for its horse races.

BALSAN ESTABLISHES CHANEL IN A MILLINERY

Life at Royallieu seems to have satisfied Chanel for about three years. Around 1908, though, she began to tire of some aspects of life there. Having had a hard childhood, she appreciated her easy existence, and she was very glad not to have to take care of herself, but she had come to feel that she was wasting her time. She wanted to find something more fulfilling to do, a meaningful project, and to make some money on her own. She began to talk once more of trying to become a singer. Her friends discouraged this, though, perhaps having realized that, while she possessed

MILLINERY

The art of millinery, or hatmaking, is a dying one, and even the word has almost passed out of the English language. Unlike the women of Chanel's time, who wore them every day, most modern women don hats only to keep warm when the temperature drops or to shield their eyes from the sun. A century ago, European and American women of all ages and classes wore hats whenever they left the house. The idea of female modesty at the time required that women cover their hair, as well as other parts of the body, such as the arms and the ankles. (Men, too, customarily wore hats, until the mid-1960s.) Thus the hat was deemed an essential part of every outfit.

Poor women might own just a single simple hat, but well-to-do women purchased many and preferred those that were elaborately decorated with blossoms and feathers. The day of the department store—a large store selling a wide range of goods, organized by department—was just beginning, and shops tended to be smaller and specialized. Women generally bought their hats from milliners, whose business consisted entirely of designing, making, and trimming or decorating hats and who often took special orders.

Like dressmaking establishments, millinery shops were often, though not always, owned and operated by women. When she became a milliner, Coco Chanel entered one of the few respectable professions open to women in her time and place.

good looks and charm, she did not have a marketable singing voice.

Balsan suggested that she begin making hats to sell. Later in her life, Chanel claimed that as a child she had lived with an aunt who liked to trim her own hats; scholars say that she never actually *lived with* an aunt, but she may well have learned some milliner's skills from her long vacations with her aunt Julia. What is certain is that during the years she lived with Balsan Chanel bought the plainest of hats at big department stores in Paris and then decorated them herself. She thought the large, heavy hats covered with flowers or feathers that were still fashionable at the time looked ridiculous. The hats she made for herself were much simpler and often adorned with nothing more than a wide ribbon or a single flower. Just as her riding outfit had done before, her hats became the talk of the neighborhood. Other women started asking her to make hats for them, too. Balsan himself seems to have believed in Chanel's talent enough to encourage it openly.

Soon after Balsan proposed the idea and Chanel expressed interest, Balsan offered to her the use of an apartment he owned in Paris. She moved soon thereafter into what would become both her home and her shop. She began by displaying just a few hats in a window, which prospective customers tried on in a very basic showroom. Socialites delighted in coming to her shop because they admired its novelty; whereas the other shops that vied for their attention were ornate and overbearing, Chanel's shop was petite and elegant. They loved her hats for the same reason—the simplicity of the designs was quite original.

Her affluent clientele included several women who had been involved with Balsan romantically in the past. These women came, in part, because at the time public meetings between former and current mistresses were socially inappropriate—and thus very exciting.

BOY CAPEL: CHANEL'S ONLY LOVE

Over time, Chanel's novel little hat business expanded until she employed four other women. Eventually she decided that her venture was successful enough that she could contemplate opening a bigger shop elsewhere. She asked Balsan to lend her money to do so, but he refused. It is unclear whether this is because funds were tight for him at the time—his horse business required constant infusions of money—or because he wanted to end his relationship with Chanel.

If the refusal was because he no longer wished to be involved with Chanel romantically, then she may have felt the same way, for it is at about this time that she became involved with one of his friends. The new man in her life was an Englishman named Arthur Capel, who was known to his friends as Boy. Capel spent as much time as possible on horseback and was recognized as a brilliant polo player. He also ran a very successful business; he owned a fleet of large ships and made a great deal of money shipping coal. Chanel seems to have been involved with both men for a while before breaking off her relationship with Balsan, who apparently bore her no ill will for doing so.

In her long life, Coco Chanel would have many lovers, including some immensely rich and powerful men, such as England's duke of Westminster, and several famous or influential artists and writers. She would always maintain, though, that Boy Capel was the only man she had truly loved. She and Balsan had always spent a great deal of their time together in the company of friends, rather than retreating to be only with each other, but she and Capel spent much more time alone. Their relationship seems to have been quite absorbing and very fulfilling for both of them.

Chanel clearly found Capel much more interesting than she had found Balsan. This was largely because Capel was not only a business tycoon and a polo player, but also a thinking man. An avid reader, he passed many of his favorite books on

Thomas Mitchell Peirce, image of a woman riding sidesaddle, 1905. During her time at Royallieu, riding horses with fashionable friends became a focus of Chanel's life. At the time, Frenchwomen typically rode sidesaddle in garments that Chanel found expensive, impractical, and restrictive. She designed for herself a costume much more suited to her taste, and she asked a men's tailor to make for her a pair of leather pants that ended just below the knee, called *jodhpurs*. She wore these with a loose shirt, an open collar, and a scarf for style. The effect attracted much positive attention.

to Chanel, including a great deal of classical literature and philosophy. They read Sophocles together; they attended the theater together. Through Capel she met people involved in the theater and music, and a singer and two actresses became her close friends.

Capel, for his part, had great confidence in Chanel's business acumen and sense of style, and late in 1910 he offered her the money she needed to expand her shop—the money that his friend Balsan had denied her. She immediately established herself in the Rue Cambon, a busy street in the center of Paris on which were located other fashionable boutiques and millineries. The city's laws required shop owners to state what they sold for the public record; she registered as a milliner. Capel's investment was the only part he had in the business, which Chanel ran without his help or guidance.

Chanel's hats became more and more popular, especially after her friend Gabrielle Dorziat wore some of her work in a theatrical performance. The play's program acknowledged Chanel for providing the hats and generated new business for her. By this time, Chanel was in her late twenties and had begun to think of expanding her business to include designing clothing. Never one to sketch designs, she kept many ideas in her head for new clothes she thought would sell; but she was not yet ready to act on her plan.

DEAUVILLE

For three years, Chanel devoted herself to the shop in the Rue Cambon—and to Boy Capel, with whom she spent an enormous amount of time, talking about the books they read and the ideas they encountered out in the world.

In the summer of 1913, Capel offered to fund her in a second shop in Deauville, a very fashionable French resort town on the Atlantic coast. Capel knew from experience that the wealthy from all over Europe and the United States flocked there to vacation every summer. He took Chanel there and bought her a shop in the very chic Rue Gontaut-Biron, where she sold hats and sportswear, all of her own design. Since the shop was located on the sunny side of the street, Chanel had a white awning installed over its wide plate-glass window, and on the awning appeared the word *Chanel* in huge block letters. Thus was one of her trademarks born—this block *Chanel* is still used today as one of the company's logos.

Chanel's business did not occupy all of her time. She and Capel became regulars on the Deauville social scene, where they often went to dinner together and attended parties and many horse races. She was a spectator at his polo matches. They attracted a great deal of attention, in part because they were lively people who engaged in animated conversation on a wide range of subjects, but also because they were an attractive couple. Slim, blond Capel was an extremely handsome man, and Chanel's very dark hair and exceptionally pale skin gave her an unusual beauty.

Chanel's mode of dress also caused commentary, as more and more often she refused to dress as other women did. At a time when most women wore very elaborate dresses over undergarments so confining they made movement difficult, Chanel eschewed corsets and girdles and wore clothing that was loose and moved freely. Unlike other women, she appeared *comfortable.* She made some of her clothing herself, including long skirts that enabled her to take large steps. Sometimes she wore clothing she borrowed from Capel's closet, too, and she especially liked his sweaters and jackets.

For a time, Chanel and Capel remained known only to a select set of people. But then the chic couple caught the eye of a famous caricaturist called Sem. Having noticed them at polo matches, he drew a cartoon that depicted Capel as a centaur, carrying off Chanel. Reproduced widely in magazines and newspapers, the drawing became famous. From that point on, Chanel's face and name were recognized

High society at Deauville, 1924. Deauville was a hotspot for the international elite in the early twentieth century, and the fashionable visited public spaces like this one to "see and be seen." Men's clothing was still largely in the Edwardian style popular before World War I, but women's clothing had become far more innovative. The woman in this picture has adopted the sleeveless box style, with a raised hemline, clean lines, and an off-balance hat. She seems conscious of herself as art.

by thousands not just in Deauville and Paris, but all over France and Europe as well.

WAR LOOMS

During these years, while others noticed that the world seemed to be changing very rapidly, Chanel was so focused on her relationship with Capel and her business that she seems to have spent little time, if any, thinking about current events. France had long been in a period known as La Belle Epoque, an era in which the wealthy grew wealthier and had plenty of time for leisure. Some even complained that life had become too easy and therefore tedious. In France and other countries, though, it had been a difficult period for the working class, who had to struggle to make ends meet. Many became radical. They wanted to see society changed, so wealth would be more evenly distributed and ordinary people would have more influence on their governments.

Elsewhere in Europe, there was political upheaval. In June of 1914, the heir to the throne of Austria-Hungary, Archduke Franz Ferdinand, and his wife were visiting Bosnia, which Austria had recently annexed. A young nationalist heaved a bomb into their automobile as they drove through Sarajevo, killing them. In the years prior to the assassination, the countries of Europe had entered into secret alliances. The assassin had ties to the neighboring country of Serbia, which was allied with Russia. In turn, Russia had alliances with France and Great Britain. Within weeks, World War I began. By 1917, Great Britain successfully pushed the United States to join the war on its side. The Allies—Great Britain, France, Russia, and the United States—would fight Austria-Hungary and its very powerful German ally in an attempt to prevent the Central powers from expanding their empires.

The war dramatically changed life in France from the moment its people began to prepare for war. Men joined the military in droves. For a time, it seemed as though the war would have a very adverse effect on Chanel's business. Deauville was deserted as people cut short their vacations to return to their homes. Her setback was short-lived, however; Chanel's business would only grow from this point on. She was about to introduce women to a new way of dressing that they would consider perfect for the times.

4

Chanel Becomes a *Couturière*

1915–1923

How many cares one loses when one decides not to be some*thing*, but to be some*one*!

—Coco Chanel, quoted in
This Week, August 20, 1961

When the many people who had lived in Deauville for only part of the year fled back to their homes at the beginning of World War I, some had only a short distance to go, generally to Paris or another big city, such as Lyons. Others had come from much farther away and had to travel hundreds or even thousands of miles under adverse circumstances to return to Russia, for example, or the United States. These wealthy tourists had frequented Chanel's shop and so, with their departure, her business suffered.

Chanel's shop in the Rue Cambon. On the left awning is the classic double-*C* Chanel logo, said to have appeared originally on the sign above Coco's grandfather's tavern. The lettering of the Chanel name is an example of Chanel's own style—bold, clean lines that make a single statement.

BACK IN BUSINESS

Chanel and Capel lived in Paris for a time, but like everybody else who could, they packed and moved out of the city. The population of Deauville swelled once more as the rich flocked back to the resorts they loved. They took refuge there throughout the war. Many of them still had a great deal of money to spend, and so Chanel's business flourished once more. It grew even more rapidly when Capel gave her the money to move her business from Deauville to Biarritz, an even tonier resort town. In the new shop, she sold not just hats but a new line of clothing, borrowed from the unique look she'd created for herself over the years.

Poirot, the leading designer of the day, had taken a few tentative steps towards liberating women's bodies, showing clothes without corsets underneath, but in general, rich women still always wore very formal clothing. Active by nature, Chanel sometimes simply bought or borrowed men's clothes to develop her casual style. She liked wearing wide-legged sailor pants on boats, for example. (Because of this, some fashion historians credit her with creating the craze for bell-bottoms.) Keeping with the nautical theme, she wore on top of them a striped maillot—knit shirt—and a pea jacket and beret.

When she designed and sewed clothes for herself, she

RESORT LIFE

In the late nineteenth century, the cities of Europe (and elsewhere) were very unpleasant places to live during the summer, as there existed no air conditioning and sewage systems were inadequate. Those families who could afford to do so escaped the swelter and the smell by retreating to the countryside or a resort town. The stretch of southern coastal France known as the Riviera, with its refreshing breezes, was a choice location. The wealthy also liked to go to the many resorts located in western France, on the Atlantic Ocean.

In that era, nobody went to the seaside to actually play in the water; swimming was not yet a popular sport, and there certainly was nothing like windsurfing or jet-skiing. Nevertheless, in towns like Deauville, Biarritz, St.-Tropez, and Cannes, there was plenty to do during the warm months. Tourists often came to stay in these places for weeks or months at a time. They entertained themselves by exchanging visits, shopping, spending time in restaurants and cafés, and promenading—parading up and down a fashionable avenue or boardwalk in order to see always chose comfortable fabrics and loose shapes. Clothes like these were what her clientele bought. Customers liked them for three reasons: First, as it was war time, women felt compelled to make sacrifices, eschewing elaborate designs and fancy trims. Second, they appreciated the fact that Chanel's clothing enabled them to dress themselves—many of Poirot's clothes, for example, had so many small buttons up the back that they required the assistance of a maid. Third, they simply found her clothing attractive.

By this time, according to Ernestine Carter's *The Magic Names of Fashion*, Chanel had "discovered her greatest asset: that she was one of nature's arbiters—all she had to do was

and be seen. Many resort cities had polo grounds, casinos, and racetracks where greyhounds or horses ran. They also boasted a very active nightlife: There were concerts and plays to attend and nightclubs to visit. People also went to these places hoping they might glimpse or even meet the aristocrats and royalty who often summered in the fanciest locales.

Coco Chanel probably never visited a resort before she began her relationship with Étienne Balsan. Balsan certainly took her to resorts, although they likely would have gone for the races rather than other forms of entertainment. She and Boy Capel would later spend a great deal of time at resorts. A very dynamic and attractive couple, Chanel and Capel caught the public eye, and tourists returning home remembered and gossiped about them. This early "word of mouth" aided in the success of Chanel's later business ventures; if Chanel never reached the resorts, she almost certainly never would have achieved fame.

be herself, wear what she liked to wear, and women would follow her." (Carter, 56) She and her seamstresses created outfits one by one.

In 1916, when she used jersey in her collection, she started
a new trend that continues to this day. The supple fabric had
been used mostly to make underwear and socks, but she used
it for a body-hugging suit with a short skirt and an army-style
jacket. Years later she would state that she had done her part for
the war effort by providing women with the simpler clothes
they needed in a time of hardship. She shunned ostentation.

In 1917, the war ended when Germany and Austria were
defeated. In the postwar years, life was grim in Germany.
People had to do without, as German industry and the German
economy were ruined. This would begin a very grim period in
Russian history, as well. However, life was very different in
the rest of Europe and the United States. In those places,
the economy was strong, which meant that young people
in particular had a great deal of time to spend in leisure
and money to spend on luxuries.

A SHOP IN THE CENTER OF PARIS

When Capel's wartime duties ended—shipping goods for the
Allies—Chanel closed the Biarritz shop and she and Capel
moved back to Paris. She opened a shop on the Rue Cambon,
in the center of Paris near the famous Tuilerie Gardens.

Chanel set a trend in 1917 when she bobbed her hair,
cutting it short as a signal that "she alone was ready for
the changing world . . . after the war." (Richards, 15) Some
historians say she was the first woman to do so, but in truth
several women bobbed their hair, all around the same time.
Still, Chanel definitely stood out in France.

The postwar years were a good time for Chanel's business.
Profits from the new shop were so high that she soon had
enough money to repay Capel every franc he had given her to
establish her shops. At age 33, she was independent, a woman

of her own means who could pay her own way. She was the sole owner of a successful business with 60 employees, which was exceptional in her time and place; there were very few, if any, other women in France who were successful entrepreneurs on this scale. Other women did own shops, but they were generally much smaller. Other female-owned businesses, such as brothels and typing agencies, were also typically small. This was the situation around the world.

In her personal life, Chanel suffered during the postwar years, due to Capel. The war had made Arthur Capel and Company even more successful than previously. Coal became an immensely valuable and important commodity and Capel owned a large number of the cargo ships that transported coal. He also became involved in French politics, even though he was an Englishman. Georges Clemenceau, the president of France, began to draw on Capel's expertise in business.

Capel began to think much more of his position in society. He was descended from a good family (he was the namesake of Arthur Capel, earl of Essex, a very important statesman in the seventeenth century) even though, like Chanel, he'd been born out of wedlock. Wanting to cement his status as a wealthy and powerful gentleman, he decided it was important that he marry. It seems certain that he was in love with Coco Chanel, but he did not consider marrying her because she lacked breeding—in other words, she did not come from a family of aristocrats. He wanted a wife whose parents were of the British gentry.

CAPEL MARRIES ANOTHER WOMAN

To this end, Capel began to woo other women who were heiresses to titles and fortunes. Eventually he proposed to the daughter of the British Lord Lovat. She accepted him, apparently knowing nothing of his relationship with Chanel, which he fully intended to continue. Capel's marriage produced one child, a daughter born in April of 1919.

Capel's marriage was a huge blow to Chanel. For months afterward, she suffered from deep depression. Her friends worried because she no longer seemed animated at all. Perhaps in part to escape his memory, she moved to a villa she rented at St. Cucufa, a small town with a spectacular view of Paris. She made changes in her business as well, moving her Paris shop to an even better location on the same street—her new address, 31 Rue Cambon, would be where the shop would stay. (Today, there is still a Chanel boutique there.) She was registered as a *couturière*, rather than as a milliner. This formally signaled what would be her focus from that point on: designing clothes.

Her spirits improved, however, because Capel did in fact maintain their relationship, sneaking away from his family to spend time with her. She suffered new anguish when, perhaps intending to see her, he embarked on a trip in his car to the south of France and was killed in a horrific car crash on December 21, 1919. (He left her 40,000 British pounds in his will, one indication that he felt deeply for Coco Chanel.) The news left her devastated. Once again, she spent months in seclusion, rarely speaking to anybody else. She bought a new villa at Garches, which she used at first primarily as a retreat. Over time, it would become a gathering place for trendsetters in the Parisian cultural scene.

MISIA SERT INTRODUCES CHANEL TO A NEW CIRCLE OF FRIENDS

Over a period of two years, Chanel had developed a friendship with a Polish woman named Misia Sert. An excellent musician in her own right (as a young woman she been trained as a concert pianist), Sert was an immensely wealthy married woman who counted among her friends many innovative artists—in the broadest sense of the term—and writers. Today Sert is best remembered because her portrait was painted by such famous artists as Renoir and Toulouse Lautrec.

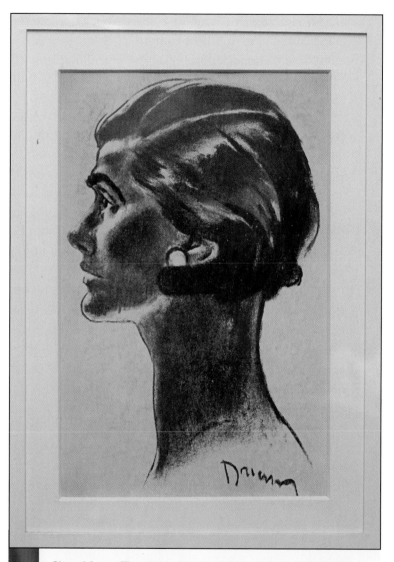

Chanel in profile. Life in France was dramatically different after World War I, and Chanel's sense of comfortable clothing and simple style found a most receptive audience. Despite the double tragedy of Boy Capel, Chanel was beginning to move in the invigorating artistic climate of the day. She mingled freely with the artists, musicians, and *literati* of the Parisian social scene and contributed to several of their projects.

Sert introduced Chanel into new circles, to people she found interesting. In Misia's company, Chanel spent much more time going to art openings, and attending plays and ballets and other cultural events. They also traveled to Italy together. Other famous people, including Pablo Picasso, Igor Stravinsky, Jean Cocteau, Paul Reverdy, Juan Gris, Salvador Dalí, and Sergei Diaghilev, began visiting Chanel's house for long evenings of animated discussion. Diaghilev, who had lost his funding when the ruling Romanov family was deposed during the Russian Revolution, lacked the money he needed to mount a ballet he was working on with Stravinsky. Chanel funded this scandalous work, *Le Sacre du Printemps* (*The Rite of Spring*), in secret, and she seems to have served as a patron to other members of the artistic community, as well.

In the summer of 1920, Chanel began a new romance with Grand Duke Dmitri Pavlovich, a member of the Russian royal family. Pavlovich was a nephew of the former Tsar Nicholas II, and as a young man he had been accused of plotting to assassinate the controversial monk Rasputin and exiled. He was now extremely short on funds, and he moved into Chanel's house at Garches with his manservant. He was a man of quiet pursuits, and he shared Chanel's love of reading.

Chanel did not devote all her time to her new friends and interests. Her business continued to grow; by the middle of the decade, 300 people would work for her. She continued to design clothing that was simple in form, but she added more elaborate details, such as silk trim and styled buttons. Her designs became as popular in the United States and Great Britain as they were in France.

CHANEL NO. 5

It was at this time that Chanel entered a whole new field when she launched what would become her signature perfume, *Chanel No. 5*. This was a special scent designed especially for her by the accomplished chemist Ernest Beaux, a friend of

Pavlovich. Beaux did all the mixing, and Chanel sampled and commented until Beaux had found exactly the scent she wanted.

Until this time, all perfumes had been made from flowers. Beaux's new design, on the other hand, was a synthetic scent, manufactured in a laboratory from 80 different ingredients; it did not smell like flowers, and it lasted longer and was far more stable than other compounds. The other perfumes of the day faded so quickly that women had to apply them liberally if they wanted the scent to last, so they often reeked of perfume at the beginning of an evening out. *Chanel No. 5* was stable enough that women could apply only a small amount and still be assured of a lasting fragrance.

Chanel No. 5 was also unique because it was not sold in a "feminine" bottle, as most perfumes of the time were. Other perfumes were bottled in flasks shaped like flowers or cupids, or in bottles etched to appear as though they were covered in lace. Chanel sold hers in a heavy, square glass bottle in the Art Deco style, with a stopper and a simple black and white label that bore only her name and the magic number. She believed this allowed the shopper to admire the *contents* of the bottle, rather than the bottle itself. The first perfume ever to appear under a designer's name, it was destined to become a classic, and it remains popular today. (The legendary Marilyn Monroe once said that *Chanel No. 5* was all she wore to bed.)

It was not only Pavlovich's Russian contacts that influenced Chanel's designs, though; it was also the Russian cultural heritage. In the early 1920s, certainly while she was involved with Pavlovich, Chanel originated the embroidered "peasant" blouse, or *rubashka*, worn with a long, straight skirt. Pavlovich's sister even helped Chanel to produce these. The look caught on almost immediately and has regained its popularity in recent years. These and similar innovations—involving fur, for example—brought a Russian flavor to much of Chanel's work of this period.

Chanel No. 5 as it appears today. Though most perfumes of the time were made from actual flowers, *Chanel No. 5* was a synthetic compound, allowing for a subtle, stable scent with only one tiny application. The heavy, square Art Deco–style glass bottle contrasted starkly with the ornate flasks that were more common at the time. Chanel believed presenting the product in this way gave more emphasis to the contents than the package, and the perfume made the same statement that her clothing made—strong, sleek, and elegant.

Thus, in the mid-1920s, despite uproar in her personal life, Chanel reigned as an innovative designer of clothing and perfume. She was starting to have a tremendous influence on fashion. At the same time, she became part of a group of people who would change art and music forever.

5

The Empire Expands

1923–1936

Luxury must be comfortable; otherwise it is not luxury.
—Coco Chanel, quoted in *The New York Times*, August 23, 1964

Nature gives you the face you have at 20; it is up to you to merit the face you have at 50.
—Coco Chanel, quoted in *Ladies' Home Journal*, September 1956

By the mid-1920s, Chanel was well settled into her new house just outside Paris. She had begun to collect rare books, antique furniture (including many museum-quality Asian screens), and *objets d'art*, such as small sculptures. Despite friendships with some of the leading painters of the day, she bought no art to frame and hang on her walls, which she preferred to line with mirrors. Her home remained a place where artists gathered, including Stravinsky, Diaghilev, and Picasso. For a time Stravinsky, his wife, and their four children lived with Chanel at Bel Respiro.

Chanel's designs for *Le Train Bleu*. As a part of a creative community, Chanel designed the costumes for several of Jean Cocteau's plays, including the "opérette dansée" *Le Train Bleu* (*The Blue Train*). This photograph, taken in November of 1924, is from the Diaghilev Ballet Russe's production of *Le Train Bleu*. Chanel also used her success to become a patron of the arts, supporting members of the creative community, often through anonymous donations. This image shows Chanel's early sportswear designs; sportswear was an innovation that no one had yet pursued, and it liberated women in another way. From left to right are dancers Leon Woizikowsky, Lydia Sokolova, Bronislav Nijijska as the tennis champion, and Anton Dolin.

Although she continued to devote most of her energies to her couture business, she did become involved in her own way in the theater. She designed the costumes for Jean Cocteau's plays, including *Antigône* and *Le Train Bleu*—which was actually an operetta. Picasso designed sets for them. A famed choreographer named Massine directed the dancers. Chanel had become part of a creative community, a group of people who exchanged ideas. She helped bring to life other people's visions. She also continued to support creative people by secretly providing them with money.

Over time, she and Dmitri Pavlovich grew apart—he married another woman and she took another lover, the married poet Pierre Reverdy.

AN UNHAPPY PARTNERSHIP

Her fashion industry continued to grow and prosper. Parfums Chanel, the Chanel perfume company, was established in 1924. When her business became very large, she entered into a partnership with the rich Wertheimer family, who already owned the largest perfume factory in France; they took over the production and sale of *Chanel No. 5*. The business arrangement between the Wertheimers and Chanel remained unstable and volatile because she refused to sign a long-term contract with them. In the short term, though, both parties found the arrangement satisfactory, especially as *Chanel No. 5* continued to gain popularity.

Chanel No. 5 would make Chanel a millionaire, according to *The New York Times*. ("Chanel, the Couturier, Dead in Paris") Its profits soon reached the point where they would "guarantee her freedom forever." (Charles-Roux, 201) It became the world's best-selling perfume.

From 1926 to 1931, her clothing would be "resolutely English" in style. (Baudot, 5) She, and the many women who imitated her, wore sweaters and jackets cut like men's. The simple clothes, made special by being created out of luxurious fabrics, sold very well not just in France, but elsewhere. American women especially liked her couture because her clothes seemed to embody youth and freedom.

PARIS IN THE 1920S

In the years immediately following World War I, Paris was a mecca for those people interested in popular culture and the arts. Known as a place where creative people could find freedom and ignore society's rules, Paris attracted artists, musicians, and dancers. Writers, too, went to Paris, to soak up its Bohemian atmosphere and to work on their poetry, short stories, essays, or novels. Included in their ranks were the Americans F. Scott Fitzgerald, Ernest Hemingway, and Gertrude Stein, all of whom later achieved notoriety. Musicians came from all over the world to learn, play, and explore a form of music that at the time was very new—jazz. Artists experimented with perspective, leading to the birth of Cubism and other movements. Creative types from many fields met and interacted in cafés and at parties, where they began collaborations or encouraged one another to complete new works.

Coco Chanel initially became part of this creative movement through her friendship with the Polish-born patroness of the arts Misia Sert. Sert introduced Chanel to a circle of people who, like her, would gain fame while living in Paris in the 1920s. As the friend of the painter Pablo Picasso, the playwright and film director Jean Cocteau, the composer Igor Stravinsky, and the ballet impresario Sergei Diaghilev, Chanel not only discussed a wealth of ideas and watched scores of other artists at work, but also provided the artistic community with financial assistance. She was also directly involved in some of their joint projects, such as designing costumes for Diaghilev's ballets. As these artists broke the rules in their own domains, so did Chanel revolutionize the world of fashion.

Even as her clothing and perfume concerns flourished, Chanel continued to look for new ventures. She established a new line of jewelry of elaborate design, similar to the jewelry that society women wore to balls or when they were presented at court. Only sometimes did her pieces include the real jewels her rich clients were used to—often she used fakes. Her creations always looked opulent, but discreet, with clean lines, subdued decoration, and beautiful color. Her jewelry was at the forefront of the Art Deco style popular in 1925, a style echoed throughout her trademarks. She began to have costume jewelry manufactured on a large scale.

One year later, she again revolutionized women's wear with a very simple design: She created for her fashion show a plain dress, in the most basic of all colors—black. Spare but elegant, this was described as the "little black dress," a phrase that has passed into the English language. Chanel had introduced the concept of one dress that could be dressed up or down and could thus be worn by fashionable women on all types of occasions, from going to work to dining out. The genius of her idea was recognized immediately, as indicated by the comparison of her 1926 dress to the Ford, the first car to become universally popular.

THE DUKE OF WESTMINSTER

Chanel's fame increased. Fashion magazines on both sides of the Atlantic gave her more and more coverage. She also achieved a new sort of celebrity after 1925 when, having broken off her relationship with Reverdy, she began a new, highly publicized romance with Great Britain's duke of Westminster. Their very intense relationship lasted for five years. The duke of Westminster, who also held the title of Prince of Wales and whose father was the king of England,

Chanel with the duke of Westminster. Chanel and the duke of Westminster enjoyed an intense, highly publicized romance that lasted for about five years. Although there was talk of marriage, the duke's engagement to the daughter of Lord Sisonby in April of 1930 meant the end of his involvement with Chanel. Chanel herself claimed to have rejected his proposal. The couple is shown here at the Grand National in the early days of their courtship, in March of 1925.

was the richest man in all of England. With many homes and more than one yacht to his name, he was a man of leisure who delighted in entertaining.

Chanel had long ago left behind the aching poverty of her childhood and the stage in her life when men supported her; thanks to her own hard work and business acumen, she had accumulated a fortune and was able to buy herself whatever she wanted. Yet with him she saw an even grander way of life, perhaps the grandest of them all. She entered a rarefied stratum. He liked her company and they spent a great deal of time together, traveling extensively. They sailed aboard his yachts and motored to various cities and resorts, visiting places like Monte Carlo. She lived with him for weeks at a time at his different estates in England.

The duke of Westminster was very much in the public eye. Gossip columnists began to link his name with Coco Chanel's in newspaper reports published all over the world. This made Chanel even more famous than before. People came to know her not just as a dress designer, but as a member of the social elite. After she purchased a new country estate of her own, named La Pausa, magazine articles were written about the house, describing how she decorated it in a very sumptuous style. By 1928, one biography says, she had become the unofficial first lady of France, meaning that she was the Frenchwoman best known all over the world.

Throughout her relationship with the duke, she remained at the forefront of fashion, presenting two fashion shows a year. Her designs were publicized by fashion magazines. Leading photographers of the day had her sit for portraits which, when published, revealed her own personal style to the public. Her name continued to be synonymous with innovation in fashion.

On one level, the public knew a great deal about her, but she worked very hard to prevent the public from learning everything. She kept her origins secret. She led the public to believe that the duke of Westminster wanted desperately to marry her but that her name was by then too valuable to lose in marriage. She is often credited with having rejected the duke with her usual flair: "There have been several Duchesses of Westminster—but there is only one Chanel!" Some scholars believe that she actually hoped he would propose, but he failed to do so. Obviously they felt deeply for one another, but in April of 1930, his engagement to the daughter of Lord Sisonby was announced and Chanel and the duke ceased to see one another.

From this point on, it seems, Chanel gave up hope of ever marrying. This did not mean she ceased to have lovers—she went right on having affairs, first reconciling with the poet Reverdy for a time. Despite the fact that she no longer appeared with the duke, she remained a celebrity. She also continued to keep secrets. One thing she kept from the public was the existence of her family. She supported her brothers, critics have claimed, so that they would not be tempted to sully her name. She may very well have felt affection for them, too, and helped them for that reason. Quietly, she helped out friends. She paid the funeral expenses of her old friend Diaghilev, for example. She also undertook some public works of charity.

HOLLYWOOD AND FINE JEWELRY
DURING THE GREAT DEPRESSION

During the Great Depression, couture became too expensive for many women, but their interest in luxurious clothing and jewelry continued. In 1931, the rising Hollywood film magnate Samuel Goldwyn invited Chanel to Hollywood to design costumes for the movies his studio made, and especially to dress his stars, who would include Katharine Hepburn, Greta Garbo, Gloria Swanson, Grace Kelly, and Elizabeth Taylor.

Marlene Dietrich in a Chanel pantsuit, 1933. In 1931, Chanel was invited to Hollywood to design costumes for the greatest stars of the day. She had no taste for the town or its people, but she did become known as a designer for celebrities. Among her clients were Greta Garbo and Marlene Dietrich; Dietrich in particular became known for a masculine sense of style.

He offered approximately one million dollars; she accepted the invitation. She sailed to New York and then made her way from there to Los Angeles, California. When she arrived in Hollywood, seemingly everybody turned out to meet her—a sure sign that her reputation had grown to international proportions.

In Hollywood she dressed Greta Garbo and Marlene Dietrich, the most popular stars of the day. Still, she did not like it, believing too many people there acted solely on their whims.

In 1932, Chanel opened in her house an exhibition of diamond jewelry she had designed. None of it was for sale. The admission fee collected from those who came to view the exhibit went to philanthropic organizations. That season, she ceased her involvement with Reverdy. Misia Sert came to stay at her house for the summer. About this time, she was working on a collection of thoughts that would appear in print a few years later. (Charles-Roux, 265)

Chanel began a new affair, this time with Paul Iribarnegaray, known as Iribe, a man of Chanel's own age. Famous as a satirical cartoonist, he had published first his own literary paper and then, in the 1920s, a magazine called *Le Mot*, which was noted for its illustrations. He went on to design furnishings, fabrics, jewels, and movie sets in a very grand style. He seems to have appealed to Chanel because he was a creator like her, not just an intellect. He drew her as the Republic for illustrations that appeared in *Le Témoin* (*The Witness*). In 1933, rumors circulated that they were about to marry.

At the time, the French economy, like that of the United States, was in depression. Many people were out of work. Laborers tried to unite to bring about change. Some became deeply dissatisfied with the French president and his government, and it seemed for a time that France might become Fascist, though this did not occur. There was unrest—a riot took place outside of Chanel's home on February 6, 1934, when 40,000 people took to the streets. That year, Chanel left her house on the Faubourg St. Honoré and took up residence in a suite at the Hôtel Ritz, one of the grandest hotels in the world. She considered it a refuge, and she would live there whenever she was in Paris for the rest of her life.

For the time being, she continued to go to La Pausa for long weekends and vacations. In the summer of 1935, she suffered a terrible blow when Iribe suddenly died of a heart attack while playing tennis on her court at La Pausa. Misia Sert arrived to comfort Chanel, who returned to work in Paris only in the fall.

By this time, like the rest of the world, Chanel thought that everything was about to change for the worse. In the early 1930s, Europe had begun to move toward war. The continent's economy suffered during the Great Depression, but Germany was hit especially hard. As the loser in World War I, its industry had been curtailed by the Allies. Many Germans resented other, richer nations, including Great Britain, France, the United States, and the Soviet Union. Fascism began to rise not only in Germany, but in Italy as well. The people there began to support a new sort of political system, one run by a dictator who maintained strict control over both the military and the economy. Benito Mussolini seized power in Italy, and Adolf Hitler became Germany's chancellor.

Trouble began to brew around the world as the super-powers tried to hold onto their colonies and expand their empires. Hitler became more and more aggressive, moving troops into the Rhineland while building up his army and air force. In France, the people elected a new government run by the Front Populaire, a coalition of left-wing groups. Communists and Socialists would soon have a majority of the seats in Parliament. Some people realized that the situation was becoming dangerous, but others did not.

CHANEL'S WORKERS GO ON STRIKE

Coco Chanel does not seem to have paid much attention to what was going on in the political arena, but she did become aware that a labor movement was beginning in France. In 1936, for the first time, workers in France were granted the legal right to form unions. Many workers joined unions, which fought for their members' rights. There were more and more strikes, as laborers refused to work unless they received higher wages or better working conditions. In May of 1936, there was what was described by Chanel's biographer as a "tidal wave" of activity, with massive demonstrations in support of labor. (Charles-Roux, 297). There were strikes in industry after industry—people in automobile factories went out on strike, followed by railway men, post office workers, miners, construction workers, taxi drivers, and bakers.

Chanel saw it as a men's movement, until it reached the textile industry. When her factory workers went out on strike, she "took it as a personal affront." (Charles-Roux, 298) It seemed as though there was a settlement, but then the women who worked in department stores walked out. Chanel believed the wages she paid to Chanel Company workers were fair. She was horrified and enraged when her employees—they now numbered 3,000—staged a sit-down strike, refusing to work. Some formed a picket line. One morning, Chanel's accountant went to her shop to do the books but found the door barred. She fled to the Hôtel Ritz, to Chanel's rooms, to express her terror.

Chanel refused to budge. She refused to see the representatives of her employees who came to see her. She went to her

Chanel in 1929. Shown here wearing her trademark pearls, Chanel was by this time leading the elite in Paris. She was introduced to a new circle of friends, and many famous people, including Pablo Picasso, Igor Stravinsky, Jean Cocteau, Paul Reverdy, Juan Gris, and Salvador Dalí, would often visit Chanel's home, enjoying interesting conversation and inspiring creative connections. This photograph was taken by the prolific celebrity photographer Alex Stewart Sasha.

shop, where she, too, was denied entry. She was reluctant to give in to the worker's demands, but she slowly realized that she had to if she wanted to create her autumn collection. She capitulated, and the women went back to work.

6

War, Collaboration, and Exile

1936–1954

Jump out the window if you are the object of passion. Flee it if you feel it. . . . Passion goes, boredom remains.
— Coco Chanel, quoted in *McCall's*, November 1965

When I hear the word *culture*, I reach for my gun.
— Attributed to Nazi leader Hermann Göring

When Chanel's workers went out on strike, she felt betrayed. She had expected them to feel such personal loyalty to her that they would work for her no matter what conditions she offered. She would have liked to fire every one of them, but she could not, for there were not enough skilled seamstresses in Paris to replace them. One reason for this was because another female designer had recently arrived on the scene, an Italian woman known only as Schiaparelli. Schiaparelli started out small, but over time she hired many of the skilled workers who might

Chanel in 1937. In the late 1930s, there was some talk from critics that Chanel's regular collections were lacking in inspiration. There was variety in her work, but she seems to have preferred the simple, classic lines that never failed her and remain popular today. She was very involved in costume design for various projects during this time, including designs for Cocteau's play *Oedipe Roi* (*Oedipus the King*) and Jean Renoir's film *Les Règles du Jeu* (*The Rules of the Game*).

otherwise have worked for Chanel. She and Chanel were quickly becoming rivals.

To a certain extent, after the strike ended, Chanel's life went back to normal. In May she attended the new Expo, or exhibit, of jewelry. She went to La Pausa for the summer, as usual. In the new year, she attended the ballet in Monte Carlo. She was seen out and about with the Grand Duke Dmitri Pavlovich, her beau of so many years ago.

Over the next three years, she continued to work. Critics have said she seemed to lack inspiration in her regular collections. This was not true of her extracurricular projects: She did the costumes for Cocteau's new *Oedipe Roi* (*Oedipus the King*) as well as Jean Renoir's film *Les Règles du Jeu* (*The Rules of the Game*).

WORLD WAR II—CHANEL CLOSES THE BUSINESS

As Chanel went about her routine, the world changed. Germany, under the dictatorship of Adolf Hitler, began building up a massive army. In 1936, Germany, Italy, and Japan signed treaties of mutual defense. Then both Germany and Japan set out to expand their empires.

In 1938, Germany formed a new, powerful alliance with Austria, assuming control of that large and rich country. Next Hitler moved to take over Czechoslovakia. The Allies ceded some of that country to Germany but, unsatisfied, Germany invaded Czechoslovakia in March of 1939. At the same time, Japan was taken over by militarists who were also dedicated to expanding the Japanese empire. They set their eyes on China.

Like much of the rest of the world's population, Chanel seems to have paid little attention to these developments. In the fall of 1938, she showed long dresses. In the spring of 1939, she showed "gypsy" dresses in blue, white, and red, the colors of the French flag. Looking back, observers remember that spring as the last one in which Europeans had time to dance. Once Germany invaded Czechoslovakia, most people came to believe that war was imminent. Millions of Frenchmen reported for duty in the military.

That summer, work slowed at the House of Chanel. First she decided not to mount a fall fashion show. Then she decided to shut down her couture house, claiming it would be closed permanently. She apparently felt no remorse over shutting down. Although she had worked very hard to disguise her feelings, she had remained angry with her workers after they settled their differences in 1936. She used her decision to shut down her business as an opportunity to break off her relationship with almost all of the remaining members of her family. By this time both her sisters had died. She had been sending her two brothers money on a regular basis but now informed them that she was financially unable to continue, even though she still had plenty of money—far more than anyone realized.

Although she stopped designing clothing and accessories, the shop on the Rue Cambon remained open, selling only one item—*Chanel No. 5.* Her signature scent remained popular. In fact, its sales increased throughout the war, partly because soldiers—first Germans and later Americans—bought it while on leave in Paris.

The German army, continuing its campaign of expansion, invaded Poland on September 1, 1939. Both Great Britain and France had military treaties with Poland and were committed to defend it, so on September 3, they declared war on Germany. The Soviet Union, also bound by treaties, joined their alliance. (The United States at first remained neutral, but would later join the fight on the side of the Allies.) Germany, of course, had its own alliance, the Axis powers.

The war started slowly, but in 1940, Hitler unleashed what he called his *blitzkrieg,* or "lightning war." His troops occupied Denmark and Norway. His tanks then rolled across the Netherlands, Belgium, and Luxembourg. All the British troops who had been posted in the area fled across the English Channel to the safety of home. Now France stood alone. On June 22, as the German army advanced toward Paris, the French government surrendered. German soldiers occupied Paris. France was divided in two, with two separate governments. The north of France was German-occupied, while central and southern France remained free and was governed from Vichy. A resistance movement started, but it faced incredible odds.

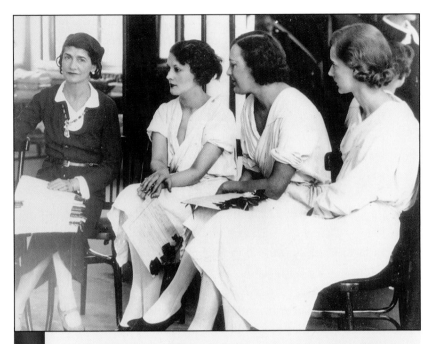

Chanel with workers in Paris. In 1936, as the labor movement began to gain momentum, workers in France acquired the legal right to form unions for the first time. Chanel thought of this as primarily a men's movement—until her nearly 3,000 textile employees staged a "sit-down" strike. Believing the wages she paid to her workers were fair, Chanel took the strike personally. She made the deals necessary to ensure the production of her line, but the strike did lasting damage to her relations with the workers.

Of course, the German occupation of Paris disrupted the lives of Chanel and her circle of friends. Many of them fled the city. For a time, Chanel traveled about, visiting friends in the country. Eventually she returned to the Hôtel Ritz in Paris, where she had lived in a luxurious suite before she closed her business. Many German officers now lived at the Ritz, in some cases forcibly removing occupants from their rooms. Some say the hotel management had put Chanel's belongings into storage and that when she returned, the accommodation she was given was the equivalent of a storage closet. Chanel biographer Axel Madsen provides another version of the story, in which a German general espied her trunks, which were stenciled with her name, and immediately ordered them brought up to his room because of his regard for her talents. (Madsen, 237)

OCCUPIED PARIS

After she got settled, Chanel telephoned Misia Sert, who scolded her for choosing to live among the German military leaders, believing that she was unwittingly sending a signal that she supported the Germans. Chanel still valued Sert's opinion, but she stayed put.

On one of the following days, she went to 31 Rue Cambon, where she witnessed brisk sales of *Chanel No. 5* as German soldiers purchased bottles for the wives and sweethearts they had left behind. Twelve other couture houses still had their doors open, but she did not choose to reopen hers. She spent her days reading and talking to friends, sometimes going out. Paris was still an exciting city. The presence of so many German officers during the German occupation meant there was a vibrant night life, and cultural activities continued. Galleries counted to mount art exhibitions.

In occupied France, new laws barred Jewish people from holding public office. Soon they would be barred from owning businesses, too. Many French were captured and sent to German occupation camps. Among them was Chanel's nephew, Andre Palasse. According to one of her biographers, Chanel decided to intervene on his behalf. She approached a German named Hans Gunther von Dincklage, who asked her to call him by his nickname, Spatz.

Von Dincklage, born to a German father and an English mother, had been raised in Germany. His government had sent him to Paris as a diplomat years earlier, in 1928. What he did in Paris during the war years is a subject of debate. Some say he was a member of the German intelligence. Others believe he was in fact a spy for Great Britain. What is clear is that he had some influence—he persuaded a German officer named Momm to make arrangements for Palasse to come back to France and be given charge of a textile factory.

CHANEL'S AFFAIR WITH VON DINCKLAGE

Chanel apparently found von Dincklage very charming. Despite a difference in their ages—she was about 12 years older than he—they became lovers. The winter of 1940–1941 was a hard one for Parisians, as it was particularly cold and fuel was in extremely short supply. Her relationship with von Dincklage must have made Chanel's life considerably easier, for he would have been able to buy food, for instance. A young friend of Misia Sert's named Boulos Ristelhueber kept a diary of these days, and he recorded occasions when Chanel's friends went to visit her at the Ritz. They talked and sang and ate and drank together. It is reasonable to assume that they also sometimes attended the films, plays, and concerts that were still available in the city.

Chanel passed most of her days in this way until 1943, when she embarked on three new and very different projects. First, she designed the sets for a revival of Jean Cocteau's *Antigône*. Then she tried to seize control of her perfume business from Pierre Wertheimer, but she failed, despite both the fact that laws in occupied France would have favored her over a Jewish person and the fact that the Wertheimers had fled France for the United States. Chanel tried to persuade the government to give her control of the company—a major argument being that she was Aryan—but the Wertheimers quickly arranged for a non-Jewish man to buy the company, pre-dating the documents to make it look as though the sale had occurred before the German occupation. The family bribed a German official to approve the sale, and Chanel was defeated.

Also at this time, Chanel undertook a controversial

Winston Churchill, his son Randolph, and Coco Chanel. While involved with the duke of Westminster, Chanel had the opportunity to become aquainted with Winston Churchill, then chancellor of the exchequer. Years after this photograph was taken of the pair hunting with Churchill's son in January of 1928, Chanel participated in a German-sponsored program of espionage, one that involved Churchill, to bring about an early end to World War II.

secret mission on behalf of the German government. The previous winter, the German offensive had begun to slow. Chanel had heard German officers talking about the end of the war, and of *how* it might end. Before the war, when she was involved with the duke of Westminster, she had become acquainted with Winston Churchill. She conceived an inspired idea: She would try to meet with Churchill and negotiate a separate peace between Great Britain and Germany. That summer, she approached Momm, who took the idea to his superiors.

People high up in the German government wanted to let Winston Churchill know that they were hoping to negotiate a separate peace, even though the idea enraged Hitler. Through Momm, Chanel received permission to undertake what was called *Modelhut*—an operation whose name suggests a hat of *haute couture*. Chanel was acquainted with the British ambassador to Spain, who was based in Madrid. She agreed to go to that city, taking with her an old friend, Vera Bate, who was not only closer to Churchill than she was, but also a member of the Windsor family, the royal family of Great Britain. The plan was for Chanel to write a letter requesting a meeting with Churchill and then to work with Vera Bate to see the letter transmitted. In November of 1943, claiming to be considering a new location for the Chanel Company, the two women traveled to Madrid; they found British diplomats difficult to persuade. Churchill had been expected there, but he became gravely ill and did not appear—so Chanel never had a chance to meet with him. Apparently, she went on to meet with authorities in Berlin, but there was no new plan involving her.

The situation in France changed radically when the Allies landed at Normandy on June 6, 1944. They fought their way across the country, but slowly. The Germans did not pull out of Paris until late in August. When they went, Spatz joined the retreat. Chanel stayed behind and watched French General Charles de Gaulle march into the city in triumph.

CHANEL IS ARRESTED AS A COLLABORATOR

In the weeks that followed, as the government resumed, those who had collaborated with the Germans were tracked down. Chanel's affair with von Dincklage had been public, and in September, she was arrested by the French police and charged with having been a collaborator. She was in jail for only a few hours before the charges were dropped. The reasons why are not known, although some people speculate that Churchill himself interceded on her behalf. Some say that she had to be released for fear she would betray secrets the British government did not want revealed. Other women who were found guilty of collaboration suffered dire punishments, including being paraded nude through the streets of the city.

Although her name had officially been cleared, Chanel seems to have felt humiliated. She decided to leave Paris and went first to Clermont Ferrand, the capital of the French province of Auvergne, a large but isolated city nestled amongst volcanic mountains in the south of France. Obtaining British and American visas, she continued to move about, to London and elsewhere. Later she moved farther afield.

She obtained Spatz's release from a POW camp and then went hiking with him in Lausanne, a fashionable town in Switzerland that over the years had been home to many other exiles, including some deposed kings. The two did some skiing in the Alps and met up with Paul Morand, who interviewed Chanel for a book he proposed to write. Morand's impression was that Chanel was feeling depressed at this time; perhaps life away from the fashion industry was taking its toll.

In 1947, Chanel began legal proceedings against the Wertheimers for control of her perfume business. They finally reached a settlement, and after the suit she signed a formal contract with the Wertheimer family for the first time. After the war, Pierre Wertheimer had returned to France and reassumed control of the company that he had ostensibly sold. He treated Chanel with generosity, despite her machinations against him. From that point on, she received a royalty of 2 percent on the gross sales of all fragrances that carried her name. This amounted to roughly one million dollars per year—and it made her fortune.

She returned to Paris for a time in 1950 because Misia Sert was dying. (By this time, Spatz seems to have fallen by the wayside.) In that same year, she began a collaboration with Gaston Bonheur on a book about her life. Bonheur soon bowed out of the project; Andre Fraigneau stepped in but then also

COLLABORATORS

When Hitler's Nazi Germany, intent on expanding to become a vast empire, sent soldiers to invade and occupy northern France during World War II, some French citizens committed what could be seen as an act of treason by collaborating, or cooperating, with the enemy.

Some French people helped the German army by selling supplies or providing information on the whereabouts of Jews or resistance fighters. Frenchwomen who became involved in romances with Germans during the occupation were also labeled collaborators. Many of these so-called collaborators cooperated with the army not because they were Nazi sympathizers—supporters of the Nazi regime—but simply because they wanted to make money or to protect themselves.

When the German army was forced to flee France as its defeat and the end of World War II neared, the French government that resumed power charged and arrested collaborators. Coco Chanel was one of those arrested. It is not clear why she was not found guilty of the charges against her. When she discussed the matter later in her life, she declared that she was innocent of collaboration, guilty only of falling in love with a man who happened to have been born in Germany. (She also repeatedly pointed out that her lover, whom she did not name, was only half-German, having had an English mother.) Many believe that it was intervention on Chanel's behalf by British officials, rather than arguments such as these, that prevented her from going to jail.

Chanel was fortunate. Other women who were found guilty of collaboration with the Nazis underwent humiliating punishments, including having their heads shaved and being paraded naked through city streets.

gave up, concluding that Chanel was too uncooperative to make the project feasible.

Walter Schellenberg, whom Chanel had known in Paris, had been an assistant to Heinrich Himmler, Adolf Hitler's second-in-command, during the war. He was also a chief of the SS, the Third Reich's main information-gathering service. After the war, he was tried at Nuremberg for war crimes and imprisoned. He began work on his memoirs after his release, and he is known to have contacted Chanel by telephone in 1951. He had completed a rough draft of his memoirs when he died in 1952, and Chanel paid his widow a large sum of money to have her name removed from them. From that point on, aside from funding Schellenberg's funeral, she talked very little in public about the war years. She did admit that she'd had an affair with a German, but she rationalized her actions; she reportedly once explained to Cecil Beaton, "Really, sir, a woman of my age cannot be expected to look at his passport if she has a chance of a lover." (Madsen, 262)

Twice during these years, rumors circulated that Chanel was about to come out of exile. The first of these came about when Schiaparelli closed her house in 1950; then newspapers published similar rumors in February of 1954. Chanel declined to comment, but apparently she actually was considering reopening her business. The possibility may have come to her when Wertheimer told her in 1953 that sales of her perfume had begun to slip, even if only a little bit. She may have feared her fortune was in jeopardy.

Back in the Rue Cambon

1954–1971

There is no time for cut-and-dried monotony. There is time for work.
And time for love. That leaves no other time!

—Coco Chanel

In self-imposed exile in Switzerland, Coco Chanel stayed out of the limelight for years. Her name occasionally appeared in the papers, but to a much lesser extent than before. According to *Time* magazine, in the early 1950s, "her name still had 'disgraced' attached to it." (Sischy, 2) Despite her best efforts, rumors still circulated that she had been a Nazi sympathizer. Always sharp-tongued, she was criticized for anti-Semitic remarks she made; she has also been called a homophobe.

A woman who never owned very much clothing, Chanel seems to have continued to wear only things she had designed herself in earlier times. Presumably she kept abreast of what

Chanel in April of 1954. For a number of reasons—financial concerns, boredom, disgust with the fashions of the time—Chanel decided, after 15 years in exile, to reopen her shop on the Rue Cambon. She returned to Paris from Switzerland and established a residence above the salon in which this picture was taken. In the years that followed, Chanel focused on her work and had very little in the way of social interaction. She worked in preparation for the November showing of her comeback collection, challenged by critics but finally embraced by the public.

was going on in fashion—she lived among people who could afford couture outfits, after all, and she must have noticed what they wore. But she herself ceased to have an influence on fashion—the look she favored was nowhere to be seen.

A new French designer named Christian Dior was the hottest name, as creator of what had been called the New Look. He and Chanel shared a love for luxurious fabrics, but that was basically all they agreed upon. His very elaborate styles contrasted with her simple fashions in the extreme. Observers believed that women liked his stiff, overblown, very elaborate dresses because they signaled that there was no longer a need to conserve or dress down. People had been exhausted by the war. Now they felt in the mood to celebrate.

CHANEL RETURNS TO BUSINESS

Chanel surprised everyone when she returned to Paris in 1953 with the intention of returning to the fashion scene the following year. Over the years, biographers have given three different reasons for her return. Edmonde Charles-Roux believed that she simply had become bored with her life of leisure. Another reason given is that she had become worried about money. Pierre Wertheimer reported to her that sales of *Chanel No. 5* had recently fallen off, for the first time in 30 years. In fact, the decrease in sales was quite slight and *Chanel No. 5* remained one of the most popular of all perfumes (as it does today). Nevertheless, she became so concerned, according to Axel Madsen, that she decided to generate new income. She herself claimed that she was so disgusted with the styles of the day that she felt compelled to return. It seems likely that she may have been influenced by more than one of these factors.

Whatever her compulsion, Chanel decided to hire a new staff and reopen her workroom and the shop on the Rue Cambon. Having sold La Pausa, she returned to live full-time in Paris. She had an apartment above the boutique where she took some meals and occasionally entertained, but she slept across the street, in her old suite at the Hôtel Ritz. From this point until she reached the age of 70, work filled almost all of Chanel's time; she lived only for her business. She had no more romances. By this time, many of her longtime friends had died. She kept in contact with a few people but in general lived a very isolated existence. She lived within walking distance of her shop, and seldom left the neighborhood. The servants who cooked and cleaned for her were her most frequent companions. She did little for pleasure, outside of work, but collect *objets d'art* and read.

BACK AT WORK

At work, she remained a perfectionist who paid close attention to every little detail of the clothes that bore her name. Fifty years earlier, clothing had been made of silk, wool, or cotton. Now there were many more options available, including synthetic fibers. Chanel experimented with many of the new fabrics. She was also interested in using new production techniques to develop a ready-to-wear line. In the past, each of her outfits had been made by hand. Now she considered how to get her clothes into the hands of women most effectively, and sought a first-class manufacturer to reproduce her designs.

For months, she went to the workrooms every day. When her seamstresses presented work to her, she had models slip on the prototypes and then went to work with her scissors, altering the garments until each achieved a shape that pleased her. She was extremely concerned with how her clothes moved. She wanted them to be not just luxurious but comfortable.

Chanel was still sole owner of her couture house. She could have gone to the Wertheimers to get all the start-up money she needed for her comeback collection, but decided instead to take a different approach. She made sure in advance that the American fashion magazines would feature her line, and took advance orders for her creations. Then she took just half of the cost of the collection from the perfume company.

In November of 1954, she showed her comeback collection, which featured garments predominantly navy and black in color. The first model down the runway wore a cardigan suit made of black jersey. Tweed suits were followed by dresses with wide skirts and fitted bodices, and then by evening wear. In keeping with the mood of the day, she used soft and feminine fabrics in her gowns, including satin and lace. Still, they looked very different from Dior's designs, because they featured no boning or padding.

Critics panned the collection, but retailers found it attractive and placed orders for Chanel's new line. In the words of one commentator, "[Their] experience told them that simplicity would be the way of the future." (Richards, 1954) There were in fact plenty of women who had the money to buy the very elegant clothes of Dior and his sort, but there was a growing population of young married and working women who wanted easier clothing. They wanted classic styles that they could wear throughout the day and into the night.

THE CHANEL SUIT

Slowly it became clear that Chanel's comeback was a success. Over the next 15 years, she developed a range of new trademark pieces that today are regarded as classics. Most notably, she developed what seemed like an infinite series of variations on what is identified to this day as the Chanel suit. Very simple in terms of shape, it consisted of a cardigan jacket and a knee-length skirt. What made it work was the incredible attention she paid to detail. She designed every variation on it precisely, checking over and over again to make sure every detail was exactly as she wanted it. She had it made out of lush, expensive fabrics that felt wonderful and appeared especially beautiful up close. She tailored it to flatter a woman's figure, making sure it allowed the wearer to move, to walk briskly, to sit and stand up in a graceful fashion. It worked so well that many powerful women adopted it as their uniform. One of these was Helen Lazarett, the editor of *Mademoiselle*.

To complete the rich look, Chanel created the two-tone slingback, a quilted shoulder bag, and heavy jewelry. She also continued to design both casual wear and evening clothes. Her little black dress reappeared in many guises. It remained a classic, as did her perfumes, something women reached for time and time again.

The richest women went to her boutiques in Paris to be fitted by Chanel for clothing. Her clientele included so many celebrities that when asked, "Who do you dress?" she replied, "Ask me rather who don't I dress." (Baudot) Women who

The signature Chanel suit. Timeless classics in the
Chanel collections include "the little black dress" and
"the Chanel suit." Each involves a simple style, developed
in a series of seemingly infinite variations. The two-piece
suit consisted of a simple cardigan jacket and knee-length
skirt. Chanel's eye for detail to both style and function
ensured the design's reputation as a classic in all its
many forms. The suit shown here is in rose houndstooth
check with golden belt; it was first presented in Chanel's
autumn/winter collection in Paris in July of 1969.

could not afford her expensive line flocked to buy knockoffs, or imitations. This did not bother her in the least. When asked about copying of her work, she stated that she found it very flattering to have her designs copied. She did not want to imitate fashions she saw in the street; she wanted to be the person whose ideas made it down to the working class.

By 1957, she was back on the top of her game. That year, Christian Dior died, but there were other very successful designers working, some of whom were more than 50 years younger than Chanel. These included Pierre Cardin and Yves Saint Laurent—who assumed Dior's mantle when he died, despite the fact that he was still only 20 years old.

THE FASHION OSCAR

Chanel's influence was publicly acknowledged in 1957, when the famous Neiman-Marcus department store invited her to come to Dallas, Texas, to receive what has been described as the Fashion Oscar. Her trip was covered by magazines and newspapers. *Mademoiselle* magazine ran her photograph on its cover. A promiment newspaper article described her as "sensationally good-looking, with dark-brown eyes, a brilliant smile, and the unquenchable vitality of a twenty-year-old." (Madsen, 245)

Chanel greatly enjoyed a private dinner party at the home of Diana Vreeland who, while watching her talk to Helena Rubinstein, was struck by the great strength of her personality. She commented that both Chanel and Rubinstein had come from nothing and accumulated great wealth, and suggested that both had experienced true happiness, "at least when they were in power, at the wheel, and when they were running everything." (Madsen, 245)

In the years that followed, Chanel continued to work long hours on every workday, despite her advanced age—in 1963, she turned eighty. She herself did nothing to celebrate. Others noted the occasion, however: Great Britain's *Vogue* did a piece on her that was accompanied by a photograph of a stern-looking Chanel wearing her scissors, attached to a ribbon, around her neck.

The years that followed were turbulent, both in the United States and Europe. Many young women adopted a whole new look. They liked "the pop look." They also chose clothes that looked ethnic. While Chanel liked some of what they wore, she continued in the main to produce more of her trademarks. Rich and powerful women continued to regard her as one of fashion's leading designers despite her advancing age. Diana Vreeland, Princess Grace of Monaco, and Jackie Kennedy were

THE FASHION OSCAR

In 1957, Coco Chanel took a trip to the United States to receive from Stanley Marcus the Neiman Marcus Award for Distinguished Service in the Field of Fashion. In the eyes of the style-conscious, this award, commonly known as the Fashion Oscar, is an important recognition. It comes from Neiman Marcus, a very exclusive Dallas department store that is most famous for its Christmas catalog, which features very expensive and luxurious presents, some of which are one-of-a-kind.

Chanel often refused to accept such awards. She took offense when she was referred to as a genius, since she regarded her success as the result of her hard work rather than her innate sense of style. This award pleased her though, perhaps because she believed Stanley Marcus saw her as the hardworking perfectionist she was. In his announcement, she was referred to as the most influential designer of the century. Her trip to the United States was heavily covered by the press, including newspapers and fashion magazines. This clearly demonstrates the high regard in which American women, in particular, held her.

Chanel receives the "Fashion Oscar" from Stanley Marcus, September 9, 1957. Though many younger designers had begun to gain recognition and popularity during Chanel's comeback years, by 1957 she had reestablished herself at the top of the field. Her trip to Dallas, Texas, to receive a reward described as the "Fashion Oscar" from the Neiman-Marcus department store was covered by newspapers and magazines such as *The New York Times* and *Mademoiselle*.

often photographed in Chanel suits and evening gowns. The outfits worn by these greatly admired women were copied, but knockoffs did not cause Chanel's own business to decline. By 1968, she had more than 400 employees. *Time* magazine estimated that the House of Chanel brought in more than $160 million every year. (Madsen)

A BROADWAY SHOW BASED ON CHANEL'S LIFE

The public remained fascinated with Chanel. Rumors flew that she was a lesbian. As she aged, she became the subject of even more magazine coverage. Interviews with her were taped for television broadcast. In the mid-1960s, the Broadway producer Frederick Brisson asked Chanel's permission to mount a Broadway musical about her. It would be an homage to her personality and her style.

Chanel had wanted the play to be about her early years, but when movie star Katherine Hepburn agreed to star in it (despite the fact that she could not sing), Hepburn's age mandated that the musical start with Chanel's comeback. In early 1969, Hepburn flew to Paris to meet Chanel. She expressed trepidation: "Here I was, supposed to be meeting this great figure of fashion—and look at me! I've worn the same coat for forty years!" (Madsen, 315) Nevertheless they hit it off, perhaps because they were both strong, independent women who had succeeded in a man's world.

Cecil Beaton designed the sets and costumes for the show. Previn wrote the score. Paramount Pictures bought the film rights for $2.75 million, $900,000 of which went to mount the show—for that time, a huge amount of money. In fact, as of that time, *Coco* "was the most expensive show in Broadway history." (Madsen, 314)

Chanel had promised that she would come for the premiere, but her health did not permit her to attend. She finally had to admit that she had begun, in some ways, to decline. She had developed arthritis—sometimes her hands felt so stiff that she could hardly move them. She suffered from a variety of other maladies, as well. Still, she continued to work.

8

Chanel's Legacy

Some people think luxury is the opposite of poverty. It is not. It is the opposite of vulgarity.

—Attributed to Coco Chanel

Look for the woman in the dress. If there is no woman, there is no dress.
—Coco Chanel, quoted in *The New York Times*, August 23, 1964

In 1970, the world appeared to be in the midst of change. In the United States, young people seemed to question nearly all their elders' ways. The situation was much the same in Europe. Young women joined the feminist movement, hoping to change the world. Coco Chanel might have been expected to support this movement—after all, from an early age, she had been a trailblazer herself, making her own way and finding for herself a place in the world. Nevertheless, she did not join the

Chanel: a lifetime of influence in fashion and culture.
Coco Chanel died of natural causes at the age of 87.
News of her death and celebration of the influence of her
life received attention around the world. She had always
been an outsider of one kind or another, but it was exactly
that difference from others, that uniqueness, that made her
designs so sensational. She made her mark by liberating
women from the unnecessary constraints of "someone
else's" fashion.

cause, even though "her work is unquestionably part of the liberation of women." (Sischy, 1)

Chanel started by creating clothes that were comfortable. At the end of her life, she was still creating clothes that were comfortable, but had also, in an age when fashion changed very rapidly, imbued her clothes with a timelessness that allowed women to wear them into boardrooms. While the world around her changed at a rapid rate, Coco Chanel led a simple life, following a quiet routine and spending much of her time working. Reviewers and socialites continued to flock to the fashion shows she mounted twice yearly. When the new year began in 1971, she was finishing preparations for the spring show she planned to put on a few weeks later. On January 8, a Friday, she left her workrooms late, as usual. The following day she spent at home, reading and talking with a friend. Recently, her health had been good, so her maid was surprised when she found that Coco Chanel had died in her sleep, on the morning of January 10, 1971.

When she died of natural causes at the age of 87, Chanel's obituary appeared in newspapers all over the world. *The New York Times* described her as "one of the greatest couturiers of the 20th century," and then went on to laud her for her keen business sense, noting that at one time she managed four separate enterprises—her couture house, a textile factory, perfume laboratories, and a workshop where costume jewelry was manu-factured. ("Chanel, the Couturier, Dead in Paris") In the days and weeks that followed, more newspapers and magazines published long retrospectives on her life. They reflected on the profound influence she had on fashion for more than 60 years.

According to her wishes, her funeral was held at La Madeleine, one of the oldest and most ornate churches in Paris. Her models—some of whom sobbed—filled the front pews. Hundreds of other people, including French government officials, crowded into the church, while the streets outside were packed with people wishing to catch a glimpse of her coffin and the celebrities in attendance. After the service, her body was shipped to Switzerland for burial.

In the months that followed, her vast fortune was disposed of, the bulk of it willed to servants and a foundation. By the time of her death, Chanel had broken off virtually all ties with her family. Her death did not mean the end of the House of Chanel, however. Coco Chanel had not been its sole owner. Her longtime partners, the Wertheimers, assumed complete control of the company. Her many employees kept right on working. The spring collection she had been working on was shown in February, as planned. The audience's reaction was favorable— orders poured in, as always.

For close to 15 years, the Chanel line of clothing, jewelry, accessories, and fragrances continued to be created by the designers who had worked under Chanel in her last years. Twice a year, they continued to mount fashion shows in Paris, where the company's headquarters remained. There were Chanel boutiques all over the world. Chanel products continued to sell, although the House was no longer regarded as particularly innovative.

In 1983, the Wertheimer brothers hired German-born designer Karl Lagerfeld to head the company as chief designer. He remains in that position today. For 20 years, he has paid homage to Coco Chanel while simultaneously making his own mark. He has changed the company in some major ways. For example, the House of Chanel now sells not only couture but also ready-to-wear clothing, which means that many more women can afford to purchase clothing bearing the Chanel label.

Today, Chanel, the company, remains in the forefront of fashion and continues to prosper. The company continues to acknowledge the influence of Chanel—its website, for example, features many photographs and a biography of her. Women, including celebrities, continue to buy the clothes she herself made, as collectibles. "A Chanel suit . . . is relatively immune to the vicissitudes of fashion," *Forbes Magazine* said, reflecting on the fact that other designers go in and out of fashion among collectors, but interest in Chanel remains constant. (Rohleder)

It is not just the Chanel label that lives on. So does the legend of Coco Chanel, the woman. Chanel remains a subject of public fascination. Although she had talked from time to time of collaborating with an author on a biography, nothing was published during her life—the two individuals she permitted to start work on a biography both abandoned the project because

Karl Lagerfeld. The dynamic Karl Lagerfeld, shown here with his trademark sunglasses and fan, was hired in 1983 as the chief designer of the House of Chanel, and he continues in that position today. This photograph was taken on October 6, 1985, at the opening of an exhibit in Rome that reviewed his two decades of work with the competing house Fendi.

she wanted too much control over what they said. Authors thinking of writing an unauthorized biography of her found it extremely difficult to collect enough accurate information.

Several biographies appeared in the decade following her death, though. The first, written by an old friend, told the story of Chanel as she herself had presented it, with all the fictions,

CHANEL IN MUSEUMS

The general public often sees couture as clothing that is both absurd and outrageously expensive, but many see it as a fine art. In fact, many of the world's leading art museums include a costume or textile division that collects couture. Chanel is well-represented in the most prestigious collections.

For example, the renowned Costume Institute at the Metropolitan Museum of Art in New York City, which includes more than 75,000 items spanning seven centuries, includes two Chanel pieces on the list of its top 50 treasures: a 1927 coat that curators especially prize because it shows both Chanel's minimalist touch and the era's fascination with the Orient, and a 1938 suit left to the museum by the glamorous Diana Vreeland, long-time editor of the American magazine *Vogue*. Chanel's creations are also found in couture museums in France and Asia. Amy de la Haye, a curator at London's world-class Victoria and Albert Museum, so highly regards Chanel and her work that she wrote a scholarly book focusing on Chanel's achievements.

In 2000, the Metropolitan Museum of Art planned to mount a show devoted to Chanel's work, but problems arose after it agreed to let the Chanel Company donate $1.5 million to sponsor the exhibit. The current head designer at Chanel, Karl Lagerfeld, wanted a great deal of control over what would be shown in the museum, and the resulting arguments finally caused the museum's director to cancel the exhibit. When the announcement was made in June of 2000 that the exhibit had been canceled, many opinion pieces appeared in the press concerning corporate sponsorship of museum exhibits in general.

Andy Warhol's take on Chanel No. 5. The lines and overall style of the Art Deco bottle were as revolutionary as the rest of Chanel's work; like the fragrance, the bottle was a total departure from all that had come before it. Along with costume jewelry and other inexpensive innovations, *Chanel No. 5* enabled women of lower incomes to feel chic, and public enthusiasm made Chanel's fortune. The influence of this simple, bold style was so profound that the artist Andy Warhol (1928–1987), who painted icons of consumer culture in the 1950s and 1960s, included the bottle along with Coca-Cola and Campbell's Soup. Warhol, a leader of the Pop Art movement who had begun his career in advertising, painted this bottle seven times.

including a poignant story about the death of her mother from tuberculosis. This book would later be the basis of a movie. Charles-Roux published a series of books about Chanel in the mid-1970s, in which she claimed to set many facts straight.

As the years went by, other biographies regularly appeared. Books were written about Chanel the *couturière* and her jewelry collection. She was also featured in a book about the greatest women collectors of all time and another about courtesans, in which she is distinguished by the fact that she was a courtesan who went on to become a success in her own right, as a businesswoman.

In 2000, the Metropolitan Museum of Art in New York City planned an exhibit that would focus on Chanel. At the last moment, the show was canceled because of funding problems—the Chanel Company had offered to give the museum an enormous sum of money to help with its costs, but in return wanted a great deal of control over what went into the exhibit. This created a lot of talk in the museum world, concerning ethics.

Even thought the exhibit was canceled, Chanel remained known. The year 2000 was a time of reflection, when many historians looked back at the century just past. Coco Chanel was recognized several times over as one of the most important women of the twentieth century; this recognition came to her not just because of her innovative designs but because she was an enormously successful entrepreneur. *Time,* for example, included her on its list of the 100 most influential people of the twentieth century. She was the only fashion designer who made the list. In *Time*'s article, Ingrid Sischy summed up Chanel's significance by saying (emphasis added), "The clothes she created changed the way women looked *and how they looked at themselves."*

Beginning by dressing herself as she wanted, Coco Chanel had, over several decades, developed such influence that she helped women look and feel confident and capable. The individual items she created fell out of fashion, but her general look did not. Her life reflected a phrase often attributed to her: "Fashion goes; style remains."

Chronology

1883   Gabrielle Chanel is born in Saumur, France, on August 19.

1895   Chanel's mother dies at the age of 33, and her father, Albert Chanel, abandons his children. He sends his sons to work on a farm and his daughters to be raised and educated by nuns.

1903   Chanel is given the nickname Coco while she is a singer at a cabaret.

1904   She becomes a courtesan, the mistress of a wealthy Frenchman named Étienne Balsan, and lives at his chateau.

1908   Chanel opens a hat shop in a Paris apartment owned by Balsan. Socialites consider her hats very chic and flock to buy them.

1910   Arthur "Boy" Capel, her new lover, gives Chanel the money to buy a shop of her own in the fashionable Rue Cambon in Paris.

1913   With more money given her by Capel, Chanel opens a new shop in the resort town of Deauville, to sell couture.

1914   Chanel closes the Deauville shop and establishes a new one in Biarritz. Her business will suffer, but only for a time, when World War I breaks out.

1916   An American magazine, *Harper's Bazaar*, features a Chanel design for the first time. When she repays Capel for his investment in her business, she achieves financial independence.

1919   Chanel is devastated by the death of Capel in a car accident.

1924   In partnership with the Wertheimer family, she begins to sell *Chanel No. 5*, which will become one of the most famous perfumes of all time.

1926 Chanel introduces the "little black dress."

1928 After she begins a new romance with the duke of Westminster, one of the richest men in the world, Chanel enters a British phase. Her shows feature tweed, jackets, and sweaters.

1936 Chanel is infuriated when her workers go on strike. She agrees to pay them more money but remains resentful.

1939 When World War II breaks out, she closes her couture house, but sales of her perfume continue.

1943 Hoping that she can help bring an end to the war, Chanel attempts to meet with British Prime Minister Winston Churchill.

1944 Chanel chooses to leave France and go into exile in Switzerland after she is accused of collaborating with the Germans during the war. (She readily admits to having had a romance with a German man in Paris.)

1954 After years away, she returns to the fashion industry, reopening her *maison de couture*. Her comeback is triumphant.

1971 Coco Chanel dies of natural causes in her apartment at the Hôtel Ritz.

Sportswear (1913), a whole new concept, grew from Chanel's habit of borrowing comfortable clothes from her male friends in order to move about more freely on horseback and in general.

Chanel No. 5 (1921–1923), is referred to as the first "modern" perfume, both because it was the first to draw on more than flowers for its scent and because it was the first to be sold worldwide.

The "little black dress" (1926) represented Chanel's idea that, rather than buying a new outfit for every important occasion, women needed simple, elegant clothing that they could dress up and down as they wished; *Vogue* compared this to Ford's Model T in terms of its impact on the (fashion) world.

Costume jewelry (1928) enabled women of all classes to accessorize basic outfits; before Chanel began to sell costume jewelry—copies of jewels given to her by the duke of Westminster—wealthy women wore only the real thing.

The Chanel suit (re-introduced in 1954) became so well known as a symbol of luxury that it was featured in an episode of *The Simpsons*; generally inspired by French military uniforms and English hunting fashions.

Baillèn, Claude. *Chanel Solitaire.* Quadrangle/New York Times Book Co., 1974.

Baudot, Francois. *Mademoiselle Chanel.* Chanel, Inc., 1992.

Carter, Ernestine. *Magic Names of Fashion.* Weidenfeld & Nicolson, 1980.

"Chanel No. 1" [obituary]. *Time* (January 25, 1971). Available online at *www.time.com/time/time100/artists/profile/chanel_related.html.*

"Chanel, the Couturier, Dead in Paris" [obituary]. *The New York Times* (January 11, 1971). Available online at *www.nytimes.com/learning/general/onthisday/bday/0819.html.*

Charles-Roux, Edmonde. *Chanel and Her World.* Knopf, 1981.

Cocteau, Jean. *My Contemporaries.* Chilton, 1968.

Gidel, Henry. *Coco Chanel.* Flammarion, 2000. [In French.]

Haedrich, Marcel. *Coco Chanel: Her Life, Her Secrets.* Little, Brown, 1972.

Madsen, Axel. *Chanel: A Woman of Her Own.* Henry Holt, 1990.

Ouston, Philip. *France in the Twentieth Century.* Macmillan, 1972.

Richards, Melissa. *Chanel: Key Collections.* Welcome Rain Publications, 2000.

Rohleder, Ann. "Art of Collecting Vintage Clothes." Available online on the *Forbes* website, *www.forbes.com/2001/08/22/0822connguide.html.*

Sischy, Ingrid. "Chanel." *Time 100: The Most Influential People of the Twentieth Century: Coco Chanel.* Available online at *www.time.com/time/time100/artists/profile/chanel.html*

Charles-Roux, Edmonde. *Chanel: Her Life, Her World, and the Woman Behind the Legend She Forged Herself.* Knopf, 1975.

De la Haye, Amy. *Chanel: The Couturiere at Work.* Overlook Press, 1996.

Golbin, Pamela. *Fashion Designers.* Watson-Guptill, 2001.

Morris, Edwin L. *Scents of Time: Perfume from Ancient Egypt to the 21st Century.* Bulfinch Press, 2000.

Richards, Melissa. *Chanel: Key Collections.* Welcome Rain Publications, 2000.

Wallach, Janet. *Chanel: Her Style and Her Life.* Welcome Rain Publications, 1998.

Chanel [the official website of the House of Chanel]
www.chanel.com

Vogue Paris: Bienvenue Chez Coco [Virtual tour of Chanel's apartment in the Rue Cambon]
www.vogueparis.com/fr/cult_visites.asp?IDRUB=303

The Metropolitan Museum of Art: The Costume Institute
www.metmuseum.org/collections/department.asp?dep=8

The Costumer's Manifesto
www.costumes.org

Ministry of Foreign Affairs [France]: The Great Names of French Couture: Coco Chanel
www.france.diplomatie.fr/label_france/ENGLISH/DOSSIER/ MODE/cha.html

The HyperFashion Who's Who: Chanel
www.unibw-muenchen.de/campus/WOW/v1041/hyper/chanel.html

Fashion Net
www.fashion.net

Fashion Planet
www.fashion-planet.com

Fashion-Era: Fashion History and Costume Eras, Victorian to Haute Couture
www.fashion-era.com

Index

Index

Index

and Lagerfeld as chief designer
after death of Chanel, 19, 97
and move to 31 Rue Cambon,
52
and new fabrics, 87
profits of, 92
ready-to-wear line for, 87, 97
and second comeback collection,
17-18
and selling only perfume during
World War II, 74-75, 77
and Wertheimers controlling
after death of Chanel, 96-97
Rue Gontaut-Biron, Chanel's shop
on, 42-43
Russia
and Chanel's affair with
Pavlovich, 54, 55
influence of on Chanel's designs,
55
and Revolution, 54
and World War I, 45

*Sacre du Printemps, Le (The Rite of
Spring)*, 54
Sailor pants, Chanel designing, 48
Saint Laurent, Yves, 90
St. Cucufa, Chanel renting villa in,
52
Saumur
Chanel born in, 22
Chanel's childhood in, 25, 27
French cavalry in, 25
Schellenberg, Walter, 83
Schiaparelli, 72-73, 83
Sem (caricaturist), 43-44
Serbia, and World War I, 45
Sert, Misia, 52, 54, 67, 68, 77, 78,
81
Shoes. *See* Pumps, Chanel designing
two-toned
Shoulder bags, Chanel designing,
17, 88

Shows, 64
after Chanel's death, 97
and first comeback collection,
12-14, 16-17, 87
and gypsy dresses, 74
and long dresses, 74
in old age, 96
and second comeback collection,
17-18
and World War II, 74
Silk trim, Chanel using, 54
Sischy, Ingrid, 21-22, 101
Sisonby, Lord, duke of Westminster's
engagement to daughter of, 65
Soviet Union, and WWII, 75
Sportswear, Chanel designing, 17, 88
for Biarritz shop, 47-50
for Deauville shop, 43
Stravinsky, Igor, 21, 54, 58
Strike, of Chanel's workers, 15, 69,
71, 72-73, 75
Suits, Chanel designing
after Chanel's death, 97
and first comeback collection,
12-14, 87-88
jersey for, 50, 87
style of, 17, 88
Swanson, Gloria, 65
Switzerland, Chanel's self-imposed
exile in, 12, 14, 15, 81, 83, 84-86
Synthetic fibers, Chanel experi-
menting with, 87

Taylor, Elizabeth, 65
Témoin, Le (The Witness), 67
Theater, Chanel's involvement in,
59-60
Time, and Chanel as among the
100 most influential people of
twentieth century, 19, 101
Trademarks
as Art Deco, 62
block *Chanel* as, 43

Index

page:

13: Courtesy of the Library of Congress, LC-USZ62-85843

18: © Bettmann/CORBIS

21: © Richard List/CORBIS

26: © Bettmann/CORBIS

29: © Hulton-Deutsch Collection/CORBIS

35: Courtesy of the Library of Congress, LC-USZ62-102576

41: © Swim Ink/CORBIS

44: © HultonlArchive, by Getty Images

47: © CORBIS SYGMA

53: © Massimo Listri/CORBIS

56: © ASTIER FREDERIK/ CORBIS SYGMA

59: © HultonlArchive, by Getty Images

63: © HultonlArchive, by Getty Images

66: © Associated Press, AP

70: © Hulton-Deutsch Collection/CORBIS

73: © HultonlArchive, by Getty Images

76: © Bettmann/CORBIS

79: © Bettmann/CORBIS

85: © Associated Press, AP

89: © Associated Press, AP

92: © Bettmann/CORBIS

95: © CORBIS KIPA

98: © Associated Press, AP

100: © 2003 Andy Warhol Foundation for the Visual Arts/ARS, New York/Art Resource, NY

Cover: © HultonlArchive, by Getty Images

Contributors

Ann Gaines is a freelance author who lives outside of Gonzales, Texas. She holds master's degrees in American civilization and library science from the University of Texas at Austin. She has written more than 50 nonfiction books for children, including other biographies for Chelsea House.

Congresswoman Betty McCollum (Minnesota, Fourth District) is the second woman from Minnesota ever to have been elected to Congress. Since the start of her first term of office in 2000, she has worked diligently to protect the environment and to expand access to health care, and she has been an especially strong supporter of education and women's health care. She holds several prominent positions in the House Democratic Caucus and enjoys the rare distinction of serving on three House Committees at once. In 2001, she was appointed to represent the House Democrats on the National Council on the Arts, the advisory board of the National Endowment for the Arts.